Gasoline

DATE DUE

Gasoline

Other Books in the Current Controversies Series

I Gasoline

Debra A. Miller, Book Editor

GREENHAVEN PRESS
A part of Gale, Cengage Learning

GALE
CENGAGE Learning·

Detroit • New York • San Francisco • New Haven, Conn • Waterville, Maine • London

8/12   # 777327470

Elizabeth Des Chenes, *Director, Publishing Solutions*

For more information, contact:
Greenhaven Press
27500 Drake Rd.
Farmington Hills, MI 48331-3535
Or you can visit our Internet site at gale.cengage.com

For product information and technology assistance, contact us at

Gale Customer Support, 1-800-877-4253
For permission to use material from this text or product, submit all requests online at www.cengage.com/permissions

Further permissions questions can be emailed to permissionrequest@cengage.com

LIBRARY OF CONGRESS CATALOGING-IN-PUBLICATION DATA

Gasoline / Debra A. Miller, book editor.
  p. cm. -- (Current controversies)
Includes bibliographical references and index.
  ISBN 978-0-7377-6227-3 (hardcover) -- ISBN 978-0-7377-6228-0 (pbk.)
  1. Gasoline--Prices--United States. 2. Gasoline industry--United States. 3. Energy consumption--United States. 4. Energy policy--United States. I. Miller, Debra A.
  HD9579.G5U5428 2012
  338.4'3665538270973--dc23
                                                        2012004708

Printed in the United States of America
1 2 3 4 5 6 7 16 15 14 13 12

Contents

Chapter 1: How Does Oil and Gasoline Dependence Affect the US and the World?

Deborah Gordon

Gasoline-powered cars and trucks are major producers of carbon dioxide and other greenhouse gases that cause global warming. Although transportation is responsible for nearly one-third of the carbon emissions into the atmosphere, little is being done to reduce these emissions because of the world's dependence on petroleum fuels to operate its vehicles.

Deron Lovaas and Justin Horner

America's dependence on foreign oil supplies causes American drivers economic pain in the form of skyrocketing gas prices. In 2010, US drivers in almost every state spent more of their income on gasoline than they did in 2009.

Jonathan Powers

Approximately 39 percent of the money spent by the United States on foreign oil imports goes to countries that are hostile to America. The US appetite for oil funds terrorist organizations and drives up the price of oil worldwide, providing resources to people who want to do us harm.

Chapter 2: Are Rising Gasoline Prices a Serious Problem?

Yes: Rising Gasoline Prices Are a Serious Problem

Foreword

By definition, controversies are "discussions of questions in which opposing opinions clash" (*Webster's Twentieth Century Dictionary Unabridged*). Few would deny that controversies are a pervasive part of the human condition and exist on virtually every level of human enterprise. Controversies transpire between individuals and among groups, within nations and between nations. Controversies supply the grist necessary for progress by providing challenges and challengers to the status quo. They also create atmospheres where strife and warfare can flourish. A world without controversies would be a peaceful world; but it also would be, by and large, static and prosaic.

The Series' Purpose

The purpose of the *Current Controversies* series is to explore many of the social, political, and economic controversies dominating the national and international scenes today. Titles selected for inclusion in the series are highly focused and specific. For example, from the larger category of criminal justice, *Current Controversies* deals with specific topics such as police brutality, gun control, white collar crime, and others. The debates in *Current Controversies* also are presented in a useful, timeless fashion. Articles and book excerpts included in each title are selected if they contribute valuable, long-range ideas to the overall debate. And wherever possible, current information is enhanced with historical documents and other relevant materials. Thus, while individual titles are current in focus, every effort is made to ensure that they will not become quickly outdated. Books in the *Current Controversies* series will remain important resources for librarians, teachers, and students for many years.

In addition to keeping the titles focused and specific, great care is taken in the editorial format of each book in the series. Book introductions and chapter prefaces are offered to provide background material for readers. Chapters are organized around several key questions that are answered with diverse opinions representing all points on the political spectrum. Materials in each chapter include opinions in which authors clearly disagree as well as alternative opinions in which authors may agree on a broader issue but disagree on the possible solutions. In this way, the content of each volume in *Current Controversies* mirrors the mosaic of opinions encountered in society. Readers will quickly realize that there are many viable answers to these complex issues. By questioning each author's conclusions, students and casual readers can begin to develop the critical thinking skills so important to evaluating opinionated material.

Current Controversies is also ideal for controlled research. Each anthology in the series is composed of primary sources taken from a wide gamut of informational categories including periodicals, newspapers, books, US and foreign government documents, and the publications of private and public organizations. Readers will find factual support for reports, debates, and research papers covering all areas of important issues. In addition, an annotated table of contents, an index, a book and periodical bibliography, and a list of organizations to contact are included in each book to expedite further research.

Perhaps more than ever before in history, people are confronted with diverse and contradictory information. During the Persian Gulf War, for example, the public was not only treated to minute-to-minute coverage of the war, it was also inundated with critiques of the coverage and countless analyses of the factors motivating US involvement. Being able to sort through the plethora of opinions accompanying today's major issues, and to draw one's own conclusions, can be a complicated and frustrating struggle. It is the editors' hope that *Current Controversies* will help readers with this struggle.

Introduction

> *"Although Americans are now dependent on gasoline to fuel their cars, trucks, and other transportation vehicles, gasoline was not even marketed as a transportation fuel until the late nineteenth century, when the automobile and the internal combustion engine were invented."*

Gasoline is a widely used fuel made from petroleum—a so-called fossil fuel that comes from crude oil, a mix of hydrogen and carbon naturally created from the remains of plants and animals that lived millions of years ago. According to the US Energy Information Administration (EIA), each forty-two–gallon barrel of crude oil is refined into about nineteen gallons of gasoline and the rest is used to make various other products, including kerosene, diesel fuel, heating oil, and jet fuel. Today, gasoline is the main transportation fuel in the United States; EIA says it accounts for about 66 percent of all the energy used for transportation in the United States and 47 percent of all US petroleum consumption. In 2010, Americans used 378 million gallons of gasoline each day, or about one gallon per day for every man, woman, and child in the country, and much of this gasoline comes from oil that is imported from foreign countries. Although Americans are now dependent on gasoline to fuel their cars, trucks, and other transportation vehicles, gasoline was not even marketed as a transportation fuel until the late nineteenth century, when the automobile and the internal combustion engine were invented.

In fact, crude oil itself did not exist as an energy source until 1859, when Edwin Drake dug the world's first oil well in the small town of Titusville, Pennsylvania. Drake's goal was to distill the petroleum to create kerosene for lighting homes and businesses. Finding an inexpensive type of lamp oil was an exciting prospect because at that time most people used either simple candles or whale oil for lighting, and overfishing of whales had led to a decline in the whale population and a dramatic increase in whale oil prices. Drake's discovery was the impetus for a massive oil rush that attracted speculators from around the country in search of what was called Black Gold. Later, much larger deposits of oil were discovered in Texas, and a new industry—the refining of oil for kerosene fuel for use in lamps—was created.

During these early decades of the age of oil, gasoline was viewed simply as a useless by-product, while kerosene was considered the main product. Gasoline was either discarded or sold in relatively insignificant quantities for such purposes as a treatment for lice, a way to remove stains from clothing, or as a fuel for portable stoves or lanterns. All of that changed with the advent of the automobile in the late nineteenth century. In the early 1900s, American entrepreneur Henry Ford founded an automobile company to produce vehicles with internal combustion engines that could run on gasoline. Ford's Model T car, the first mass-produced automobile, was launched in 1908. The Model T gave Americans an affordable vehicle to replace horse-drawn carriages, and it made the internal-combustion engine the standard for all future automobile manufacturers. Other forms of gas-powered transportation soon followed, including trucks, airplanes, and boats. This was the beginning of America's century-long love affair with the automobile, as well as the start of the nation's dependence on gasoline as a transportation fuel.

Largely because the United States first discovered the value of oil deposits, it dominated world oil and gas production throughout the early twentieth century. In the early days, US fields produced more than 70 percent of world oil production, and five large American oil companies eventually developed oil interests both in the United States and around the globe, including Mexico, Venezuela, and the Middle East. At the beginning of World War II (1939–45), US companies produced not only all of the oil used in America but also nearly 40 percent of oil found outside the United States and the Soviet Union. Over the years, however, US oil production declined. A prediction made in 1956 by Shell geophysicist M. King Hubbert—that US petroleum production would peak between the late 1960s and early 1970s and then begin a rapid decline—ultimately came true. The Middle East now holds the world's largest deposits of oil, although oil fields have also been discovered in many other countries.

Today, the United States is capable of producing only about 37 percent of its petroleum needs, forcing the country to rely on oil and gas imported from other nations. America now imports oil from Canada, Saudi Arabia, Mexico, Venezuela, Nigeria, Colombia, Iraq, Angola, Russia, Algeria, Brazil, Kuwait, Ecuador, Congo, and Norway. It also imports finished gasoline from countries such as the United Kingdom, the US Virgin Islands, France, Canada, the Netherlands, Norway, Germany, Russia, Italy, and Middle East nations. The US dependence on foreign sources for oil and gas is increasingly seen by many experts as a problem, for several reasons. Commentators argue, for example, that it makes the nation vulnerable to countries that are unstable or hostile to US interests and requires that it spend large sums of money on military operations to keep this oil flowing. In addition, foreign oil dependence forces the United States to compete with developing countries such as India and China, which are rapidly increasing their oil usage and are expected to create even more explosive demand in the future. And scientists note that dependence on any fossil fuel also contributes to air pollution and global carbon emissions that are causing the world climate to change in potentially catastrophic ways. Some of these factors have already led to higher US gasoline prices at the pump, which most analysts predict will rise even higher in future years.

Many experts have urged US policymakers to take steps to transition the US economy away from oil toward other types of more abundant, less polluting energy sources, such as natural gas, electricity, or renewable energy. So far, however, no viable substitute has yet been developed. The authors of the viewpoints included in *Current Controversies: Gasoline* discuss the issues surrounding the US dependence on gasoline, including the impact of this dependence, whether rising gas prices are a serious problem, whether public transportation is a viable idea, and how the United States might eventually wean itself away from fossil fuels.

CHAPTER 1

How Does Oil and Gasoline Dependence Affect the US and the World?

Chapter Preface

High gasoline prices in recent years have raised concerns regarding America's reliance on imported oil, but this is not the first time that the United States has been faced with energy issues. Energy, in fact, has been at the top of the domestic policy agenda several times since 1970, the year that experts say the United States reached its peak level of oil production. Although it is hard to imagine a time when the nation was energy self-sufficient—producing enough oil to provide for all of its needs—this actually was the case in the 1950s and early 1960s. As the country began to rely more and more on imported oil, US policymakers became increasingly worried that this could leave the country vulnerable to price increases and supply disruptions that it could not control. These worries came true and reached a crisis stage a couple of times in the 1970s, when Middle Eastern oil-producing countries sharply reduced oil exports to the United States.

The first energy crisis occurred in the early 1970s, when Richard Nixon was president of the United States. Worried about the growing US reliance on foreign oil, President Nixon initially resisted the elimination of quotas that restricted the amount of oil that could be imported from foreign countries and encouraged domestic oil producers to explore for new oil reserves. US consumption of oil, however, continued to grow, forcing Nixon to abandon the quotas in 1973 because US oil producers could not keep up with demand. The president's worst fears were realized, however, in October of that same year when members of the Organization of Arab Petroleum Exporting Countries (OAPEC)—Kuwait, Saudi Arabia, and Libya—joined with Egypt and Syria to announce an oil embargo against the United States. The embargo action was taken in response to a US decision to provide supplies to the Israeli military during the 1973 Arab-Israeli War (also called the Yom

Kippur War). The embargo halted oil shipments to the United States from OAPEC countries, and OAPEC threatened to do the same to other countries if they also supported Israel in the conflict.

The 1973 oil embargo had an immediate and devastating effect on the US economy and American lifestyles. Gas prices more than tripled almost overnight and lines at gas stations stretched for blocks. President Nixon completely banned the sale of gasoline on Sundays, extended Daylight Savings Time, and instituted a system of voluntary rationing that called on homeowners to turn down their thermostats and businesses to cut their work hours. Many schools and factories in the Northeast temporarily closed in the winter of 1973 as a cold snap hit amid the oil shortages. Meanwhile, the stock market dropped a whopping 45 percent over the next two years, as a severe recession hit the United States and the rest of the western world. The embargo was finally lifted on March 18, 1974, after negotiations of a peace deal between Israel and Syria appeared to be moving forward. However, the damage caused by the embargo continued to ripple through the US economy. Unemployment rates soared; the US inflation rate hit double digits; and the value of the US dollar sank throughout the 1970s.

The Arab oil embargo demonstrated in the most dramatic fashion possible the dangers of relying on imported oil. In response, President Nixon urged Congress to pass legislation to authorize a trans-Alaska oil pipeline to bring oil from a newly discovered oilfield in Prudhoe Bay, Alaska, to the southern United States. The Alaskan pipeline was built and in 1977 began bringing an extra 2 million barrels per day of domestically produced oil to the American market. A political scandal called Watergate focused America's attention away from the energy crisis and resulted in the resignation of President Nixon in August 1974, but later in the decade, President Jimmy Carter proposed a number of additional actions designed to reduce the nation's vulnerability to imported oil. In 1977, President Carter proposed a new energy policy, calling it the moral equivalent of war. His plan emphasized conservation, taxes to encourage people to switch to smaller cars, and a transition away from natural gas and oil to coal, nuclear power, and solar energy. He also urged the creation of a federal Department of Energy. Carter even installed solar panels on the White House as a symbolic gesture to show the nation's new commitment to becoming energy independent. Some of Carter's proposals passed the Congress, and a new Department of Energy was created, but energy companies and the American public resisted any sort of scheme for aggressively taxing gasoline and other fossil fuels. Nevertheless, domestic production increased, Americans began driving smaller cars, and US imports of foreign oil during this period were reduced.

Another oil shock occurred late in President Carter's term, caused by the 1979 Iranian revolution. Radical Islamic fundamentalists overthrew the pro-American Shah (that is, king) of Iran and installed the Ayatollah Khomeni as leader. The turmoil of the protests and revolution disrupted Iran's production and export of oil, and caused oil and gas prices in the United States to once again rise sharply. Even after the new Iranian regime settled into power, Iran's oil exports never again reached their prior levels. President Carter responded by deregulating oil prices, allowing domestic production to increase, and decreasing imports, but this did not contain prices. Once again, US drivers waited in long lines to buy gas at inflated prices and Americans worried about another recession. Unable to offer an easy solution to the crisis, President Carter was voted out of office, and Americans elected Republican Ronald Reagan to the presidency in 1980. Fortunately for President Reagan, oil exporters in places such as Mexico, Nigeria, Venezuela, and the USSR (now Russia) expanded their production, and world oil prices entered a period of decline after 1980—a period that lasted for almost two decades. As a result, Americans quickly forgot about the problem of imported oil, and President Reagan had the solar panels on the White House removed—an act that demonstrated policymakers' abandonment of energy as a top national priority.

In recent years, however, energy has once again moved onto the national agenda. This time, rising prices are linked more to rising world demand rather than to reductions of exports by oil producers. Emerging economies such as China and India are rapidly consuming more and more oil as their economies grow, even as US energy demand continues to increase as well. Oil-producing countries are struggling to increase exports to meet this demand, but this situation makes the world vulnerable to even small oil supply disruptions. The political uprisings in the Middle East in 2011, called the Arab Spring, have caused some disruptions—in Libya, for example—raising fears about the future of world oil supplies. The authors of the viewpoints in this chapter address this issue of how oil and gasoline dependence affects the United States and the rest of the world.

Gasoline Usage by the Transportation Sector Is a Major Driver of Global Warming

Deborah Gordon

Deborah Gordon is an author, energy policy consultant, and a senior associate in the Energy and Climate Program at the Carnegie Endowment for International Peace, a nonprofit organization dedicated to advancing cooperation between nations and promoting active international engagement by the United States.

The Earth's rapidly warming temperatures over the past several decades cannot be explained by natural processes alone. The science is conclusive: both man-made and natural factors contribute to climate change. Human activities—fossil-fuel combustion in transportation and other sectors, urbanization, and deforestation—are increasing the amount of heat-trapping gases in the atmosphere. These record levels of greenhouse gases are shifting the Earth's climate equilibrium.

The Role of Transportation

Climate impacts differ by sector. On-road transportation has the greatest negative effect on climate, especially in the short term. This is primarily because of two factors unique to on-road transportation: (1) nearly exclusive use of petroleum fuels, the combustion of which results in high levels of the principal warming gases (carbon dioxide, ozone, and black carbon); and (2) minimal emissions of sulfates, aerosols, and

Deborah Gordon, "Summary," *Carnegie Papers: The Role of Transportation in Driving Climate Disruption*, Energy and Climate Program, Carnegie Endowment for International Peace, Number 117, December 2010, pp. 1–2. carnegieendowment.org. Copyright © 2010 by Carnegie Endowment for International Peace. All rights reserved. Reproduced by permission.

organic carbon from on-road transportation sources to counterbalance warming with cooling effects. Scientists find that cutting on-road transportation climate and air-pollutant emissions would be unambiguously good for the climate (and public health) in the near term.

Transportation is responsible for nearly one of every three tons of greenhouse gas emissions but represents less than one of every twelve tons of projected emission reductions.

Transportation's role in climate change is especially problematic, given the dependence on oil that characterizes this sector today. There are too few immediate mobility and fuel options in the United States beyond oil-fueled cars and trucks.

U.S. and international policy makers have yet to tackle transportation-climate challenges. In its fourth assessment report, the Intergovernmental Panel on Climate Change (IPCC) [a United Nations organization created to study and report on climate change] found that the global transportation sector was responsible for the most rapid growth in direct greenhouse gas emissions, a 120 percent increase between 1970 and 2004. To further complicate matters, the IPCC projects that, without policy intervention, the rapidly growing global transportation sector has little motivation to change the way it operates, because consumer choices are trumping best practices.

Transportation Solutions Needed

Herein lies a fundamental mismatch between the climate problem and solutions: transportation is responsible for nearly one of every three tons of greenhouse gas emissions but represents less than one of every twelve tons of projected emission reductions. Clearly this sector is a major contributor to climate change; therefore, it should be the focus of new policies to mitigate warming. Government must lead this effort as the market alone cannot precipitate the transition away from cars and oil, which dominate this sector.

Policy makers need to remember four essential findings and recommendations when developing new strategies for ensuring that the United States maintains its leadership position in the global economy:

1. On-road transportation is an immediate high-priority target in the short term for reducing greenhouse gas emissions and mitigating climate change in the United States and around the globe.

2. The transportation sector is responsible for high levels of long-lived carbon dioxide (CO_2) and ozone precursor emissions that will warm the climate for generations to come.

3. The United States (and other nations) must transition quickly to near-zero greenhouse gas (GHG) emission cars and trucks, largely through low-carbon electrification for plug-in vehicles.

4. America's transportation culture must adapt to rely less on fossil fuels through technological innovation, rational pricing, and sound investments that expand low-carbon mobility choices and fundamentally shift travel behavior.

Oil Dependence Makes US Drivers Vulnerable to Rising Gas Prices

Deron Lovaas and Justin Horner

Deron Lovaas is the Federal Transportation Policy Director for the Natural Resources Defense Council (NRDC), an environmental group. Justin Horner is a policy analyst for the NRDC.

Unrest in the Middle East continues to raise concerns about our dependence on foreign oil at the same time that Americans have been suffering from the skyrocketing cost of gasoline.

To curb America's perilous oil addiction, we need effective government policies that will increase the availability and use of efficient vehicles and clean fuels, as well as promote smart growth and public transit.

This report updates the 2007, 2008, 2009, and 2010 research by the Natural Resources Defense Council (NRDC) [an environmental advocacy group] identifying the states whose citizens feel the greatest economic pain from gasoline prices and those states that are doing the most to break their addiction to oil.

Like the previous editions, this report again ranks U.S. states in two critical areas related to our nation's continuing addiction to oil. First, it calculates gasoline price vulnerability—the percentage of personal income spent on gasoline by the average driver in each state. Second, it ranks states based on their adoption of solutions to reduce their oil dependence—measures they are taking to lessen their vulnerability and to bolster America's security. The data yield some clear conclusions:

- Oil dependence affects all states, but some states' drivers are hit harder economically than others. Drivers in almost every state in 2010 spent a higher percentage of their income on gasoline than they did in 2009, and drivers in the most vulnerable states spent more than twice as large a percentage of their income on gasoline as drivers in the least vulnerable states.

- Drivers are being hit even harder right now than they were in 2010.

- While some states are pioneering solutions and many are taking some action, many states are still taking few (if any) of the steps listed in this report to reduce their oil dependence.

Drivers in every state but two were spending a larger percentage of their income on gasoline [in 2011] than in 2008—and often a good deal more.

Gasoline Price Vulnerability

NRDC's vulnerability ranking is based on the average percentage of income that states' drivers spend on gasoline. The differences are significant. In 2010, average drivers in the least vulnerable state—which for the fifth year in a row is Connecticut—spent less than 3 percent of their income on gasoline. Average drivers in the most vulnerable state—which for the fifth year in a row is Mississippi—spent more than twice as large a percentage (more than 7 percent) of their income on gasoline.

Gasoline price vulnerability generally increased from 2006 through 2008. There was a striking reversal of that trend in

2009, due largely to much lower gas prices, with drivers in every state spending a lower percentage of their income on gasoline than in 2008 (and with drivers in all but five states spending a lower percentage than in 2006). The original trend then reasserted itself, with drivers in all but four states more vulnerable in 2010 than in 2009, though not quite as vulnerable as before the 2009 blip; drivers in 45 of the 50 states were still spending a lower percentage of their income on gasoline in 2010 than in 2008.

The huge increases in gasoline prices in the first few months of 2011 have more than closed the rest of that gap. In fact, as of this April [2011], drivers in every state but two were spending a larger percentage of their income on gasoline than in 2008—and often a good deal more. In Mississippi, for instance, average drivers in April spent more than 11 percent of their income on gasoline (compared with more than 9 percent in 2008 and more than 7 percent at the end of 2010).

As the economy slowly recovers, drivers clearly remain quite vulnerable—and citizens in the high-ranking states are feeling the pinch more.

State Action on Oil Dependence: The Best and the Worst

Although some states are adopting strong measures to reduce their oil dependence, too many others are still taking little or no action.

The solutions rankings in this report are based on the range of key actions that states can take to reduce oil dependence, with particular focus on policies that can have substantial impact and can be replicated by other states.

NRDC research shows that the 10 states doing the *most* to wean themselves from oil are:

1. California

2. Oregon

3. Massachusetts

4. New York

5. New Jersey

6. Maryland

7. Connecticut

8. Rhode Island

9. Washington

10. Vermont

In contrast, the 10 states doing the *least* to reduce their oil dependence are:

1. Nebraska

2. North Dakota

3. Alaska

4. Iowa

5. Arkansas

6. South Dakota

7. Indiana

8. Missouri

9. Wyoming

10. Ohio

The failure of these 10 states—and many others—to take meaningful action to reduce oil dependence exacerbates the national security, environmental, and economic harms associated with our current transportation habits. These and other states need to be drivers of change.

The Benefits of Reducing Oil Dependence

Especially with the struggling economy, persistently high un-employment, and high gasoline and diesel prices, reducing oil dependence can yield significant benefits. These can include lowering the economic vulnerability that many residents face and creating new income from the sale of low-carbon fuels and efficient vehicles. As the recent unrest in the Middle East makes very clear, decreasing oil consumption also enhances America's national security by reducing dependence on sources of oil that are politically unstable or controlled by unfriendly national governments. In addition, reduced oil consumption decreases both air pollution and the carbon pollution that causes global climate change.

State Policies for Reducing Oil Dependence

Although the [Barack] Obama administration has taken some strong actions on energy and climate policy, states continue to be critical players in creating less oil-intensive transportation habits. State strategies include:

- *Clean and efficient vehicles.* Vehicles that cut global warming pollution reduce oil consumption consider-ably. Fourteen states, led by California, have adopted effective clean car rules. Twenty-two states have require-ments for the efficiency of the state government fleet.

- *Clean fuels.* Three states have or are developing a low-carbon fuel standard (LCFS), seeking to reduce the greenhouse gas (GHG) intensity of motor vehicle fuel, and several states have signed a memorandum of un-derstanding to explore a regional LCFS in the Northeast and Mid-Atlantic. The future of clean transportation energy, however, may be electrification. Twenty-six states have an incentive to spur greater deployment and use of plug-in hybrid and fully electric vehicles.

- *Transportation system efficiency.* An area where states can play a particularly large role in reducing oil dependence is promoting transportation system efficiency—i.e., integrating land use and transportation policies and designing them to reduce vehicle-miles traveled and promote alternatives to driving. Three states have codified or are implementing targets for reducing vehicle-miles traveled. Eight states have adopted telecommuting policies to encourage companies to enable their employees to opt out of driving. Seventeen states are taking action to encourage cars already on the road to use less gasoline by placing restrictions on idling. Sixteen states have adopted smart-growth/growth management policies to curb sprawl and reduce the associated traffic. Public investment can also be a critical strategy for states seeking to reduce oil dependence, and in 2010, New York, Massachusetts, and New Jersey led the way in prioritizing the funding of public transit through the allocation of state funds.

States that adopt cutting-edge plans to reduce oil dependence help make the nation more secure, protect drivers' wallets, and enhance global environmental health. These states' policies can serve as examples for the many states that have thus far taken little or no such action—and lead the way for national policies as well.

Federal Recommendations for Reducing Gasoline Price Vulnerability

The Obama Administration must enact effective energy and transportation policies that complement and support the actions of leading states. The Administration has made progress, but there is more to do, including:

- Raising the bar for new light-duty vehicle and heavy-duty vehicle fuel economy and carbon dioxide pollution standards, aiming for the equivalent of 62 miles per gallon by 2025 for light-duty vehicles; and

- Overhauling the federal transportation program, with prioritization and investment for maintenance and repair of our decaying infrastructure, a national oil-savings objective, more investment in public transportation, and a new infrastructure bank for new projects.

The US Dependence on Foreign Oil Funds America's Enemies

Jonathan Powers

Jonathan Powers is a US Army veteran and chief operating officer of the Truman National Security Project, a national security leadership institute that recruits, trains, and positions progressives to lead on national security issues.

The U.S. sends approximately one billion dollars a day overseas to import oil. While this figure is staggering by itself, the dangerous implications of our addiction are even more pronounced when analyzing where our money goes—and whom it helps to support.

Examine what the true costs of our oil addiction meant during the year 2008:

- *One Billion Dollars a Day Spent on Foreign Oil*: In 2008, the United States imported 4.7 billion barrels of crude oil to meet our consumption needs. The average price per barrel of imported oil for 2008 was $92.61. This works out to $1.19 billion per day for the year.

- *Our Annual Oil Debt Is Greater than Our Trade Deficit with China*: Our petroleum imports created a $386 billion U.S. trade deficit in 2008, versus a $266 billion deficit with China. This national debt is a drain on our economy and an anchor on our economic growth.

- *We Overwhelmingly Rely on Oil Imports. . .*: In 2008, we consumed 7.1 billion barrels of oil in the United States, meaning that the 4.7 billion barrels of crude oil we imported was 66% of our overall oil usage. About one out of every six dollars spent on imports by the U.S. is spent on oil, representing 16% of all U.S. import expenditures in 2008. According to calculations from the Center for American Progress, U.S. spending to import foreign oil amounted to 2.3% of our overall GDP [gross domestic product] in 2008.

- *. . . to the Detriment of National Security*: Vice Admiral Dennis McGinn, retired Deputy Chief of Naval Warfare Requirements and Programs, captured the national security dangers of our addiction to oil in 2009 testimony before the U.S. Senate Environment and Public Works Committee: "In 2008, we sent $386 billion overseas to pay for oil—much of it going to nations that wish us harm. This is an unprecedented and unsustainable transfer of wealth to other nations. It puts us in the untenable position of funding both sides of the conflict and directly undermines our fight against terror."

A comprehensive energy strategy . . . is vital to our national security, to the safety of our men and women in uniform, and to the fight against terrorism.

Our oil addiction drives up prices worldwide, pouring funds into the coffers of foreign regimes that hold anti-American sentiments, harbor terrorists, and otherwise threaten America's national security. As the Council on Foreign Relations wrote, "major energy consumers—notably the United States, but other countries as well—are finding that their growing dependence on imported energy increases their strategic vulnerability and constrains their ability to pursue a broad range of foreign policy and national security objectives."

The one billion dollars a day that Americans send overseas on oil floods a global oil market that enriches hostile governments, funds terrorist organizations, and props up repressive regimes. Former CIA [Central Intelligence Agency] Director Jim Woolsey explains it this way:

> "Except for our own Civil War, this [the war on terror] is the only war that we have fought where we are paying for both sides. We pay Saudi Arabia $160 billion for its oil, and $3 or $4 billion of that goes to the Wahhabis, who teach children to hate. We are paying for these terrorists with our SUVs." . . .

A comprehensive energy strategy—one that cuts our addiction to fossil fuels, boosts clean energy technology, and moves our nation dramatically towards greater energy independence—is vital to our national security, to the safety of our men and women in uniform, and to the fight against terrorism.

A Dangerous and Unstable Addiction

While the U.S. imports 66% of our oil, that figure includes both friendly nations such as Canada and Mexico, as well as a litany of countries whose regimes are either unstable, unfriendly, or both.

In 2008, the U.S. imported about 4 million barrels of oil a day from countries labeled "dangerous or unstable" by the State Department. Using the $386 billion total cost as cited by Vice Admiral McGinn, this means that about 39% of our oil import costs were from "dangerous or unstable" nations.

Nearly one-fifth of the oil consumed by the U.S. in 2008 (18%) was imported from countries of the Middle East and Venezuela. This total represents over one-fourth of our overall imported oil (28%) in 2008. While Venezuela is not on the State Department's "dangerous or unstable" list, it has maintained a distinctly anti-American foreign and energy policy under President Hugo Chavez. Venezuela was one of the top five oil exporters to the United States, and we imported 435 million barrels of oil from it in 2008.

Buying from Friendly Countries—or Even from the United States—Doesn't Help

The price of oil is set globally. That means that even when we buy oil from friendly countries, we drive up demand, inflating prices that enrich unfriendly countries. For instance, despite U.S. laws against purchasing oil from Iran, the global demand for oil—aided by U.S. consumption habits—helps to drive up the global price of oil and line the pockets of the Iranian regime. Oil wealth funded about 60% of the Iranian national budget in 2008. *The Economist* calculated that, in his first term, Iranian President Mahmoud Ahmadinejad benefited from "a windfall of $250 billion in oil sales." The United States currently consumes approximately one-fourth of the world's oil, inadvertently bolstering Iran's bottom line, despite the laws on the books.

Depending on oil to produce the energy that runs our nation makes America vulnerable, while simultaneously providing enormous resources to those who would do us harm.

All oil demand hurts our national security—regardless of whether the oil is produced here at home or bought overseas. Whether oil is directly purchased from nations on the State Department's "Dangerous or Unstable" list, or is bought from West Texas, U.S. demand increases global oil prices that fund our enemies.

According to testimony from Truman National Security Project Chief Operating Officer Jonathan Powers, every $5 increase in the global price of crude oil represents:

- An additional $7.9 billion for Iran and President Ahmadinejad;

- An additional $4.7 billion for Venezuela and President Chavez; and,

- An additional $18 billion for Russia and Prime Minister Vladimir Putin.

Unfortunately, even if we buy oil from a friendly country like Mexico, problem countries in the Middle East can hold us hostage by forcing up global oil prices—as Middle Eastern countries in OPEC [Organization of Petroleum Exporting Countries] have done time and time again. Buying from friendly or domestic sources does not solve our problem, because the countries with the greatest reserves—notably, Saudi Arabia—are such major producers that they set the global supply. Even if we drilled in every untapped well in America, we simply do not have enough oil from friendly countries and under the earth at home to offset OPEC's power. By staying addicted to oil, regardless of where we purchase it, we give OPEC countries the power to cripple our economy and bring America to its knees. . . .

A Better Alternative

Depending on oil to produce the energy that runs our nation makes America vulnerable, while simultaneously providing enormous resources to those who would do us harm. It is time for us to take control of our energy future, cut our dependence on oil, and defund terrorist threats with comprehensive energy legislation.

National security, military, and intelligence experts have spoken out about the need for a comprehensive strategy that takes on the destabilizing effects of fossil fuel dependence and global climate change.

"Without bold action now to significantly reduce our dependence on fossil fuels, our national security will be at greater risk," testified Vice Admiral Dennis McGinn, before a U.S. Senate panel. "Fierce global competition and conflict over dwindling supplies of fossil fuel will be a major part of the future strategic landscape."

"Moving toward clean, independent, domestic energy choices lessens that danger and significantly helps us confront the serious challenge of global climate change. Because these issues are so closely linked, solutions to one affect the other. Technologies and practices that improve energy sources and efficiency also reduce carbon intensity and carbon emissions, and, most critically, increase our national security."

A panel of 11 former generals and admirals echoed Vice Admiral McGinn's testimony in a report entitled *National Security and the Threat of Climate Change*, stating, "Climate change, national security, and energy dependence are a related set of global challenges . . . dependence on foreign oil leaves us more vulnerable to hostile regimes and terrorists, and clean domestic energy alternatives help us confront the serious challenge of global climate change."

Marine General James Mattis put it more succinctly when he was asked at a Brookings [Institution] meeting in 2007 about the most important area of research for aiding the men and women under his command: "Unleash us from the tether of fuel."

America's military leaders are not waiting to take action on the threats posed by our dependence on fossil fuels. The Defense Department considers climate change such a strategic threat that it is part of the military's long term planning. The CIA has opened a center to track the threat of climate change. The Army, Navy, Air Force and the Marines have all committed to reducing their carbon pollution.

For example, in October 2009 the Navy launched the *USS Makin Island*, a first-of-its-kind hybrid powered amphibious assault vehicle that emits less carbon and saved the Navy $2 million in fuel costs during its maiden voyage alone. The Marine Corps has even created a model Forward Operating Base (FOB) in Quantico, VA, which will allow the Marines to test a hybrid power station that is set to be deployed in Afghanistan by mid-2010.

Just as the military is innovating its own energy habits, America as a nation must do the same, with a comprehensive approach to clean energy and climate change that will have a measurable impact on these threats.

The need is immediate. "We have less than ten years to change our fossil fuel dependency course in significant ways," testified Vice Admiral McGinn. "Our nation's security depends on the swift, serious, and thoughtful response to the inter-linked challenges of energy security and climate change."

High Oil Prices Threaten
the World Economy

The Economist

The Economist *is a weekly newspaper that provides insight and opinion on international news, politics, business, finance, science, and technology.*

The price of oil has had an unnerving ability to blow up the world economy, and the Middle East has often provided the spark. The Arab oil embargo of 1973, the Iranian revolution in 1978–79 and Saddam Hussein's invasion of Kuwait in 1990 are all painful reminders of how the region's combustible mix of geopolitics and geology can wreak havoc. With protests cascading across Arabia, is the world in for another oil shock?

There are good reasons to worry. The Middle East and north Africa produce more than one-third of the world's oil. Libya's turmoil shows that a revolution can quickly disrupt oil supply. Even while [Libyan leader] Muammar Gaddafi hangs on with delusional determination and Western countries debate whether to enforce a no-fly zone, Libya's oil output has halved [in 2011], as foreign workers flee and the country fragments. The spread of unrest across the region threatens wider disruption.

The markets' reaction has been surprisingly modest. The price of Brent crude [a major trading classification of oil] jumped 15% as Libya's violence flared up, reaching $120 a barrel on February 24th. But the promise of more production from Saudi Arabia pushed the price down again. It was $116 on March 2nd—20% higher than the beginning of the year, but well below the peaks of 2008. Most economists are sanguine: global growth might slow by a few tenths of a percentage point, they reckon, but not enough to jeopardise the rich world's recovery.

That glosses over two big risks. First, a serious supply disruption, or even the fear of it, could send the oil price soaring. Second, dearer [meaning costlier] oil could fuel inflation—and that might prompt a monetary clampdown that throttles the recovery. A lot will depend on the skill of central bankers.

Even without a disruption to supply, prices are under pressure from a second source: the gradual dwindling of spare capacity.

Of Stocks, Saudis, and Stability

So far, the shocks to supply have been tiny. Libya's turmoil has reduced global oil output by a mere 1%. In 1973 the figure was around 7.5%. Today's oil market also has plenty of buffers. Governments have stockpiles, which they didn't in 1973. Commercial oil stocks are more ample than they were when prices peaked in 2008. Saudi Arabia, the central bank of the oil market, technically has enough spare capacity to replace Libya, Algeria and a clutch of other small producers. And the Saudis have made clear that they are willing to pump.

Yet more disruption cannot be ruled out. The oil industry is extremely complex: getting the right sort of oil to the right place at the right time is crucial. And then there is Saudi Arabia itself. The kingdom has many of the characteristics that have fuelled unrest elsewhere, including an army of disillusioned youths. Despite spending $36 billion so far buying off dissent, a repressive regime faces demands for reform. A whiff of instability would spread panic in the oil market.

Even without a disruption to supply, prices are under pressure from a second source: the gradual dwindling of spare capacity. With the world economy growing strongly, oil demand is far outpacing increases in readily available supply. So any jitters from the Middle East will accelerate and exaggerate a price rise that was already on the way.

What effect would that have? It is some comfort that the world economy is less vulnerable to damage from higher oil prices than it was in the 1970s. Global output is less oil-intensive. Inflation is lower and wages are much less likely to follow energy-induced price rises, so central banks need not respond as forcefully. But less vulnerable does not mean immune.

Dearer oil still implies a transfer from oil consumers to oil producers, and since the latter tend to save more it spells a drop in global demand. A rule of thumb is that a 10% increase in the price of oil will cut a quarter of a percentage point off global growth. With the world economy currently growing at 4.5%, that suggests the oil price would need to leap, probably above its 2008 peak of almost $150 a barrel, to fell the recovery. But even a smaller increase would sap growth and raise inflation.

Shocked into Action

In the United States the Federal Reserve will face a relatively easy choice. America's economy is needlessly vulnerable, thanks to its addiction to oil (and light taxation of it). Yet inflation is extremely low and the economy has plenty of slack. This gives its central bank the latitude to ignore a sudden jump in the oil price. In Europe, where fuel is taxed more heavily, the immediate effect of dearer oil is smaller. But Europe's central bankers are already more worried about rising prices: hence the fear that they could take pre-emptive action too far, and push Europe's still-fragile economies back into recession.

By contrast, the biggest risk in the emerging world is inaction. Dearer oil will stoke inflation, especially through higher food prices—and food still accounts for a large part of people's spending in countries like China, Brazil and India. True, central banks have been raising interest rates, but they have tended to be tardy. Monetary conditions are still too loose, and inflation expectations have risen.

Unfortunately, too many governments in emerging markets have tried to quell inflation and reduce popular anger by subsidising the prices of both food and fuel. Not only does this dull consumers' sensitivity to rising prices, it could be expensive for the governments concerned. It will stretch India's optimistic new budget. But the biggest danger lies in the Middle East itself, where subsidies of food and fuel are omnipresent and where politicians are increasing them to quell unrest. Fuel importers, such as Egypt, face a vicious, bankrupting, spiral of higher oil prices and ever bigger subsidies. The answer is to ditch such subsidies and aim help at the poorest, but no Arab ruler is likely to propose such reforms right now.

At its worst, the danger is circular, with dearer oil and political uncertainty feeding each other. Even if that is avoided, the short-term prospects for the world economy are shakier than many realise. But there could be a silver lining: the rest of the world could at long last deal with its vulnerability to oil and the Middle East. The to-do list is well-known, from investing in the infrastructure for electric vehicles to pricing carbon. The 1970s oil shocks transformed the world economy. Perhaps a 2011 oil shock will do the same—at less cost.

The World Energy Threat Has Only Worsened in 2011

Michael T. Klare

Michael T. Klare is a professor of peace and world security studies at Hampshire College in Massachusetts and the author of several books on energy topics.

Here's the good news about energy: thanks to rising oil prices and deteriorating economic conditions worldwide, the International Energy Agency (IEA) reports that global oil demand will not grow this year [2011] as much as once assumed, which may provide some temporary price relief at the gas pump. In its May *Oil Market Report*, the IEA reduced its 2011 estimate for global oil consumption by 190,000 barrels per day, pegging it at 89.2 million barrels daily. As a result, retail prices may not reach the stratospheric levels predicted earlier this year, though they will undoubtedly remain higher than at any time since the peak months of 2008, just before the global economic meltdown. Keep in mind that this is the *good* news.

As for the bad news: the world faces an array of intractable energy problems that, if anything, have only worsened in recent weeks. These problems are multiplying on either side of energy's key geological divide: *below ground*, once-abundant reserves of easy-to-get "conventional" oil, natural gas, and coal are drying up; *above ground*, human miscalculation and geopolitics are limiting the production and availability of specific energy supplies. With troubles mounting in both arenas, our energy prospects are only growing dimmer.

Here's one simple fact without which our deepening energy crisis makes no sense: the world economy is structured in such a way that standing still in energy production is not an option. In order to satisfy the staggering needs of older industrial powers like the United States along with the voracious thirst of rising powers like China, global energy must grow substantially every year. According to the projections of the U.S. Department of Energy (DoE), world energy output, based on 2007 levels, must rise 29% to 640 quadrillion British thermal units by 2025 to meet anticipated demand. Even if usage grows somewhat more slowly than projected, any failure to satisfy the world's requirements produces a perception of scarcity, which also means rising fuel prices. These are precisely the conditions we see today and should expect for the indefinite future.

It is against this backdrop that three crucial developments of 2011 are changing the way we are likely to live on this planet for the foreseeable future.

Tough-Oil Rebels

The first and still most momentous of the year's energy shocks was the series of events precipitated by the Tunisian and Egyptian rebellions and the ensuing "Arab Spring" in the greater Middle East. Neither Tunisia nor Egypt was, in fact, a major oil producer, but the political shockwaves these insurrections unleashed has spread to other countries in the region that are, including Libya, Oman, and Saudi Arabia. At this point, the Saudi and Omani leaderships appear to be keeping a tight lid on protests, but Libyan production, normally averaging approximately 1.7 million barrels per day, has fallen to near zero.

When it comes to the future availability of oil, it is impossible to overstate the importance of this spring's events in the Middle East, which continue to thoroughly rattle the energy markets. According to all projections of global petroleum output, Saudi Arabia and the other Persian Gulf states are slated to supply an ever-increasing share of the world's total oil supply as production in key regions elsewhere declines. Achieving this production increase is essential, but it will not happen unless the rulers of those countries invest colossal sums in the development of new petroleum reserves—especially the heavy, "tough oil" variety that requires far more costly infrastructure than existing "easy oil" deposits.

In a front-page story entitled "Facing Up to the End of 'Easy Oil,'" the *Wall Street Journal* noted that any hope of meeting future world oil requirements rests on a Saudi willingness to sink hundreds of billions of dollars into their remaining heavy-oil deposits. But right now, faced with a ballooning population and the prospects of an Egyptian-style youth revolt, the Saudi leadership seems intent on using its staggering wealth on employment-generating public-works programs and vast arrays of weaponry, not new tough-oil facilities; the same is largely true of the other monarchical oil states of the Persian Gulf.

The world can accommodate a prolonged loss of Libyan oil. Saudi Arabia and a few other producers possess sufficient excess capacity to make up the difference. Should Saudi Arabia ever explode, however, all bets are off.

Whether such efforts will prove effective is unknown. If a youthful Saudi population faced with promises of jobs and money, as well as the fierce repression of dissidence, has seemed less confrontational than their Tunisian, Egyptian, and Syrian counterparts, that doesn't mean that the status quo will remain forever. "Saudi Arabia is a time bomb," commented Jaafar Al Taie, managing director of Manaar Energy Consulting (which advises foreign oil firms operating in the region). "I don't think that what the King is doing now is sufficient to prevent an uprising," he added, even though the Saudi royals had just announced a $36-billion plan to raise the minimum wage, increase unemployment benefits, and build affordable housing.

[The 2011 earthquake in Japan] has forced Japan to increase its imports of oil, coal, and natural gas, adding to the pressure on global supplies.

At present, the world can accommodate a prolonged loss of Libyan oil. Saudi Arabia and a few other producers possess sufficient excess capacity to make up the difference. Should Saudi Arabia ever explode, however, all bets are off. "If something happens in Saudi Arabia, [oil] will go to $200 to $300 [per barrel]," said Sheikh Zaki Yamani, the kingdom's former oil minister, on April 5th. "I don't expect this for the time being, but who would have expected Tunisia?"

Nuclear Power on the Downward Slope

In terms of the energy markets, the second major development of 2011 occurred on March 11th when an unexpectedly powerful earthquake and tsunami struck Japan. As a start, nature's two-fisted attack damaged or destroyed a significant proportion of northern Japan's energy infrastructure, including refineries, port facilities, pipelines, power plants, and transmission lines. In addition, of course, it devastated four nuclear plants at Fukushima, resulting, according to the U.S. Department of Energy, in the permanent loss of 6,800 megawatts of electric generating capacity.

This, in turn, has forced Japan to increase its imports of oil, coal, and natural gas, adding to the pressure on global supplies. With Fukushima and other nuclear plants off line, industry analysts calculate that Japanese oil imports could rise by as much as 238,000 barrels per day, and imports of natural gas by 1.2 billion cubic feet per day.

This is one major short-term effect of the tsunami. What about the longer-term effects? The Japanese government now claims it is scrapping plans to build as many as 14 new nuclear reactors over the next two decades. On May 10th, Prime Minister Naoto Kan announced that the government would have to "start from scratch" in devising a new energy policy for the country. Though he speaks of replacing the cancelled reactors with renewable energy systems like wind and solar, the sad reality is that a significant part of any future energy expansion will inevitably come from more imported oil, coal, and LNG [liquified natural gas].

The disaster at Fukushima—and ensuing revelations of design flaws and maintenance failures at the plant—has had a domino effect, causing energy officials in other countries to cancel plans to build new nuclear plants or extend the life of existing ones. The first to do so was Germany: on March 14th, Chancellor Angela Merkel closed two older plants and suspended plans to extend the life of 15 others.

On May 30th, her government made the suspension permanent. In the wake of mass antinuclear rallies and an election setback, she promised to shut all existing nuclear plants by 2022, which, experts believe, will result in an increase in fossil-fuel use.

China also acted swiftly, announcing on March 16th that it would stop awarding permits for the construction of new reactors pending a review of safety procedures, though it did not rule out such investments altogether. Other countries, including India and the United States, similarly undertook reviews of reactor safety procedures, putting ambitious nuclear plans at risk. Then, on May 25th, the Swiss government announced that it would abandon plans to build three new nuclear power plants, phase out nuclear power, and close the last of its plants by 2034, joining the list of countries that appear to have abandoned nuclear power for good.

How Drought Strangles Energy

The third major energy development of 2011, less obviously energy-connected than the other two, has been a series of persistent, often record, droughts gripping many areas of the planet. Typically, the most immediate and dramatic effect of prolonged drought is a reduction in grain production, leading to ever-higher food prices and ever more social turmoil.

Intense drought over the past year in Australia, China, Russia, and parts of the Middle East, South America, the United States, and most recently northern Europe has contributed to the current record-breaking price of food—and this, in turn, has been a key factor in the political unrest now sweeping North Africa, East Africa, and the Middle East. But drought has an energy effect as well. It can reduce the flow of major river systems, leading to a decline in the output of hydroelectric power plants, as is now happening in several drought-stricken regions.

By far the greatest threat to electricity generation exists in China, which is suffering from one of its worst droughts ever. Rainfall levels from January to April in the drainage basin of the Yangtze, China's longest and most economically important river, have been 40% lower than the average of the past 50 years, according to *China Daily*. This has resulted in a significant decline in hydropower and severe electricity shortages throughout much of central China.

The Chinese are burning more coal to generate electricity, but domestic mines no longer satisfy the country's needs and so China has become a major coal importer. Rising demand combined with inadequate supply has led to a spike in coal prices, and with no comparable spurt in electricity rates (set by the government), many Chinese utilities are rationing power rather than buy more expensive coal and operate at a loss. In response, industries are upping their reliance on diesel-powered backup generators, which in turn increases China's demand for imported oil, putting yet more pressure on global fuel prices.

Wrecking the Planet

So now we enter June with continuing unrest in the Middle East, a grim outlook for nuclear power, and a severe electricity shortage in China (and possibly elsewhere). What else do we see on the global energy horizon?

Despite the IEA's forecast of diminished future oil consumption, global energy demand continues to outpace increases in supply. From all indications, this imbalance will persist.

Take oil. A growing number of energy analysts now agree that the era of "easy oil" has ended and that the world must increasingly rely on hard-to-get "tough oil." It is widely assumed, moreover, that the planet harbors a lot of this stuff—deep underground, far offshore, in problematic geological formations like Canada's tar sands, and in the melting Arctic. However, extracting and processing tough oil will prove ever more costly and involve great human, and even greater environmental, risk. Think: BP's *Deepwater Horizon* disaster of April 2010 in the Gulf of Mexico.

Such is the world's thirst for oil that a growing amount of this stuff will nonetheless be extracted, even if not, in all likelihood, at a pace and on a scale necessary to replace the disappearance of yesterday's and today's easy oil. Along with continued instability in the Middle East, this tough-oil landscape seems to underlie expectations that the price of oil will only rise in the coming years. In a poll of global energy company executives conducted this April by the KPMG Global Energy Institute, 64% of those surveyed predicted that crude oil prices will cross the $120 per barrel barrier before the end of 2011. Approximately one-third of them predicted that the price would go even higher, with 17% believing it would reach $131–$140 per barrel; 9%, $141–$150 per barrel; and 6%, above the $150 mark.

The price of coal, too, has soared in recent months, thanks to mounting worldwide demand as supplies of energy from nuclear power and hydroelectricity have contracted. Many countries have launched significant efforts to spur the development of renewable energy, but these are not advancing fast enough or on a large enough scale to replace older technologies quickly. The only bright spot, experts say, is the growing extraction of natural gas from shale rock in the United States through the use of hydraulic fracturing ("hydro-fracking").

Proponents of shale gas claim it can provide a large share of America's energy needs in the years ahead, while actually reducing harm to the environment when compared to coal and oil (as gas emits less carbon dioxide per unit of energy released); however, an expanding chorus of opponents are warning of the threat to municipal water supplies posed by the use of toxic chemicals in the fracking process. These warnings have proven convincing enough to lead lawmakers in a growing number of states to begin placing restrictions on the practice, throwing into doubt the future contribution of shale gas to the nation's energy supply. Also, on May 12th, the French National Assembly (the powerful lower house of parliament) voted 287 to 146 to ban hydro-fracking in France, becoming the first nation to do so.

The environmental problems of shale gas are hardly unique. The fact is that all of the strategies now being considered to extend the life-spans of oil, coal, and natural gas involve severe economic and environmental risks and costs—as, of course, does the very use of fossil fuels of any sort at a moment when the first IEA numbers for 2010 indicate that it was an unexpectedly record-breaking year for humanity when it came to dumping greenhouse gases into the atmosphere.

With the easily accessible mammoth oil fields of Texas, Venezuela, and the Middle East either used up or soon to be significantly depleted, the future of oil rests on third-rate stuff like tar sands, shale oil, and extra-heavy crude that require a lot of energy to extract, processes that emit added greenhouse gases, and as with those tar sands, tend to play havoc with the environment.

Recurring shortages, rising prices, and mounting discontent are likely to be the thematic drumbeat of the globe's energy future.

Shale gas is typical. Though plentiful, it can only be pried loose from underground shale formations through the use of explosives and highly pressurized water mixed with toxic chemicals. In addition, to obtain the necessary quantities of shale oil, many tens of thousands of wells will have to be sunk across the American landscape, any of one of which could prove to be an environmental disaster.

Likewise, the future of coal will rest on increasingly invasive and hazardous techniques, such as the explosive removal of mountaintops and the dispersal of excess rock and toxic wastes in the valleys below. Any increase in the use of coal will also enhance climate change, since coal emits more carbon dioxide than do oil and natural gas.

Here's the bottom line: Any expectations that ever-increasing supplies of energy will meet demand in the coming years are destined to be disappointed. Instead, recurring shortages, rising prices, and mounting discontent are likely to be the thematic drumbeat of the globe's energy future.

If we don't abandon a belief that unrestricted growth is our inalienable birthright and embrace the genuine promise of renewable energy (with the necessary effort and investment that would make such a commitment meaningful), the future is likely to prove grim indeed. Then, the history of energy, as taught in some late twenty-first-century university, will be labeled: How to Wreck the Planet 101.

CHAPTER 2

Are Rising Gasoline Prices a Serious Problem?

Chapter Overview

Toni Johnson

Toni Johnson is a senior staff writer for the Council on Foreign Relations, an independent, nonpartisan membership organization, think tank, and publisher.

Although considerable attention has been given to the role of market speculation in recent price volatility, many energy experts say demand is rising and oil supplies are increasingly constrained, which puts upward pressure on oil and, consequently, gas prices. Political unrest in the Middle East, a recovering global economy, and revived demand in the emerging markets have all contributed to rising oil prices. U.S. gas prices in the spring of 2011 were more than $4 in some places and heading toward the record highs of 2008, when gas rose to nearly $5 per gallon. The U.S. Energy Information Administration (EIA) estimates that in 2011, gas prices will cost the average consumer at least $825 more than in 2010. The U.S. debate over protecting consumers against high gasoline prices has largely focused on increasing domestic supplies or finding ways to reduce consumer demand, but there is also concern about balancing these against environmental and economic issues.

Components of Gasoline Price

The EIA, an arm of the U.S. Department of Energy, breaks the price of retail gasoline into four components: the cost of crude oil; the cost of refining and fuel-blending; federal and state taxes; and distribution and marketing expenses.

- *Crude oil*: This is the raw material used to make commercial-grade gasoline, known in much of the world as petrol. The cost of crude oil accounts for the largest percentage of what U.S. consumers pay for gas at the pump. On average, about 51 percent of every dollar spent on retail gasoline went to crude suppliers in much of the last decade, according to the EIA. In 2008, when gas and oil prices were at their highest, crude represented an average of 75 percent of U.S. gas prices and currently hovers at around 70 percent, according to April 2011 analysis from oil industry advocate the American Petroleum Institute (API). "You cannot decouple gas prices from crude prices," says one API analyst. "If you want to help the consumer at the pump, you have to make sure crude prices don't rise too much." According to the EIA, a $1 change in crude prices corresponds roughly to a 5-cent change in wholesale gasoline prices.

- *Refining*: The process of turning crude oil into products for consumer use accounts for about 7 percent of the retail price of gasoline, on national average. In the United States, refining requirements in different regions can affect gas prices. California, for instance, has the highest air quality rules, including stricter requirements for ethanol fuel-blending and sulfur content. Thus, gas prices in the West Coast region, dependent on California refineries, are significantly higher than the national average. Refining capacity can also have a price effect, as was the case in 2005 when Hurricane Katrina knocked out 20 percent of refining capacity in the Gulf region, which caused gas prices to increase.

- *Taxes*: The percentage of every dollar spent on gasoline that goes to federal or state governments has decreased in recent years. According to the EIA, taxes currently account for about 14 percent of the retail price Americans pay for gas, though this number is a national average and percentages vary significantly from state to state. The national average, including a federal tax of 18.5 cents per gallon, is 49.5 cents, but some states' gas taxes go as high as nearly 70 cents.

- *Distribution and marketing*: The combined prices of purchasing and transporting gasoline from refineries to gas stations (often via intermediary distribution points) and the costs of operating the stations account for about 10 percent of the retail price of gasoline, according to EIA data.

Oil Supply and Demand

While U.S. consumption has fallen slightly in the last five years, China, the world's second largest consumer of oil, and countries such as India and Brazil are seeing a marked increase in oil demand. Some experts say these emerging markets have played a major role in the volatility in crude prices, which in the last few years have fluctuated widely, going as high as $145 per barrel in mid-2008 before dropping to $30 and then rising again to above $100 in 2011. "As long as the emerging economies, especially the big ones, keep growing, the demand for oil will keep growing," said CFR's [Council on Foreign Relations] Michael Spence in March 2011. "So, the kind of situation we saw before the crisis in 2006 through 2008, when there was a big spike in commodity prices, could return."

Demand also has outpaced new oil investment, leading to a tightening of global production capacity. For the last few decades, Saudi Arabia, the only country with notable spare production, has attempted to act as a price buffer by raising or lowering its production in response to the market, but in recent years the country has had less room to act. Smaller margins of spare production capacity mean any potential disruptions in the oil supply have a marked effect. In 2011, the supply of oil in the Middle East became a significant concern and caused oil prices to increase as countries in the region including Libya, one of the world's top twenty oil producers, became embroiled in an ongoing pro-democracy movement. In the short term, the uprising known as the Arab Spring has instilled a new sense of insecurity in oil markets. In the longer term, what happens in the Middle East could have serious implications for oil supplies.

"If future oil demand has any hope of being met, significant investment must take place to develop Middle East and North African oil reserves," writes Paul Stevens, a senior fellow at Britain's Chatham House, noting that political uncertainty could reduce interest future investment by international oil companies. "This could mean that an impending oil supply crunch, with crucial implications for oil price levels, could come sooner rather than later."

Oil executives claim they are just as much at the mercy of market forces as consumers.

Some experts say that high oil prices are here to stay. "The age of cheap oil is over, though policy action could bring lower international prices than would otherwise be the case," International Energy Agency head Fatih Birol said in March 2011. However, CFR Adjunct Senior Fellow Atul Arya cautions against predicting permanently higher oil prices. "We can't say with confidence that prices will stay high," he says, noting that historically, prices have bottomed out with new production coming online and the softening of demand due to high oil prices and other economic factors.

Factoring in Ethanol

The EIA expects ethanol-blended fuel, currently 10 percent per volume in a gallon of gasoline (E10), to account for nearly

10 percent of U.S. consumption in 2011. A 2008 Energy Department study estimated that, on average, ethanol-blending saved the U.S. consumer anywhere from 20 cents per gallon to as much as 35 cents per gallon that year. A more recent ethanol industry report argues that in 2011, gas prices have been at least 12 cents lower than expected, thanks to the fuel additive.

But effects on prices, especially going forward, remain a topic of political debate. Some critics of corn-based ethanol, such as the environmental group Natural Resources Defense Council, argue that the 45 cent per gallon federal tax credit for blending masks the true price effect, and that the Renewable Fuel Standard, which mandates an increasing use of ethanol-blending—from nine billion gallons in 2008 to 36 billion gallons by 2022—is enough to incentivize production. Corn, a major ethanol feedstock, is also subject to commodities market fluctuations and production problems that could increase ethanol prices. Thanks to low global corn stocks, ethanol prices are at a two-year high, though still lower per gallon than crude. Still, others argue that because of its heavy reliance on corn, ethanol is in competition with food, driving up food prices, especially for the world's hungriest.

Policies to Ease Gas Prices

U.S. policymakers have implemented a number of initiatives to either increase U.S. production of oil or lower consumption, but many of these take years to have an effect and thus have had limited impact on consumers in the short term. And though lawmakers in the last decade have brought oil companies to task for high prices, oil executives claim they are just as much at the mercy of market forces as consumers.

"No one person, organization, or industry can 'set' the price for crude oil," Marvin E. Odum, head of Shell Oil Company, told the Senate Finance Committee on May 12, 2011. "Stated simply, oil is a global commodity. And oil companies are price takers, not price *makers.*" Some analysts note that though gross oil industry profits seem large, the industry's profit margin (which takes in the cost of oil production) ranks 114 out of 215 industries—making on average a little over 6.5 cents for every dollar.

Still, the [Barack] Obama administration and Democrats in Congress already have renewed attempts to end $4 billion in annual oil company subsidies, but it is unclear whether it will affect prices. On May 14, [2011] President Obama also announced new plans to aid new domestic drilling, including leasing new parts of the Gulf of Mexico and Alaska, and encouraging drilling on unused energy leases on land and offshore.

Increasing domestic drilling, proponents say, will reduce U.S. dependence on foreign oil as well as encourage lower oil prices by increasing supply. Shale oil advocates estimate production using hydraulic fracking (inserting liquids into a well to push out trapped oil) could yield as much as two million barrels a day by 2015—more than what is currently produced offshore in the Gulf of Mexico. Similarly, there is intense interest in boosting conventional offshore and deepwater production—which some argue could yield an additional two million barrels in the next five years.

Many experts contend that reducing consumption through demand-reduction policies is the biggest buffer against high gas prices.

However, such endeavors face challenges. Some projects will require oil prices to stay high to justify new investment and will take years to bring up to scale. And environmental issues such as water use and quality concerns, as well as greenhouse gas intensity, could slow development or raise costs through environmental compliance. For example, shale gas production—which also uses fracking—is under fire for water pollution concerns, and U.S. offshore production and leasing has slowed after the Obama administration imposed new environmental regulations following the four-month Deepwater oil spill [in the Gulf of Mexico] in 2010.

Other analysts say the United States does not hold enough oil to make a significant impact. "In 2009, the U.S. produced about 7 percent of what was produced in the entire world, so increasing the oil production in the U.S. is not going to make much of a difference in world markets and world prices," EIA analyst Phyllis Martin told the *Huffington Post*.

Instead, many experts contend that reducing consumption through demand-reduction policies is the biggest buffer against high gas prices. Overall, CFR's Arya says that what should be communicated to consumers by policymakers is that the world is already "thinking about what's next" when it comes to dealing with oil dependence.

The United States is already implementing new corporate average fuel economy standards, and consumers have moved toward purchasing more fuel-efficient cars. [A recent] *Scientific American* article explores demand-reduction policies, including increased use of biofuels and alternative-fueled vehicles, and attaching new crude oil or gas taxes.

Unlike API, which favors reducing current gas taxes to help the U.S. consumer, some experts see a massive increase in gas taxes—in effect raising prices even further—as the simplest way to deter consumption. The United States pays the lowest fuel tax and thus lower fuel prices than any other industrialized nation and less than some emerging-market countries, such as China.

Increases in Gas Prices Act as a Drag on the Economy

Dante Chinni

Dante Chinni is a journalist and the director of Patchwork Nation, a project of the Jefferson Institute, an independent research and education organization that studies politics, socio-economics, and culture.

Are the hopes for an economic recovery disappearing into our gas tanks? On Thursday [April 28, 2011] the Commerce Department reported economic growth had slowed to an annual rate of 1.8 percent. It had been projected to be as high as 4 percent.

There are many influences on that dip—from trade imbalances to reduced government spending—but it's hard to ignore the influence of gas prices. The numbers are dramatic. A Patchwork Nation analysis of data from GasBuddy, finds prices are up over a dollar-a-gallon compared to last year in some places—and, as is usually the case, pain has not been spread evenly.

To be clear no one has been spared a hit at the pump, but some types of counties—like the sparsely populated Mormon Outposts in the Mountain West—have seen much smaller bumps than others. And as one might expect, the big city Industrial Metropolis counties, not only have the highest prices overall, sitting just shy of $4 a gallon, they also have seen the biggest increase. A gallon of gas is more than a dollar more than it was in April 2010.

How does that translate into economic pain exactly? Directly and indirectly. A recent analysis from Deutsche Bank finds that every penny increase in average gas prices at the pump in the United States equals $1.4 billion siphoned out of the US economy.

But a lot of the real pain depends on where you live, what stage of the "recovery" your community is experiencing and your driving habits.

The Differences

The increase in gas prices has swamped the country, sparing no one. The bumps in most of our 12 county types are pretty uniform—between 92 cents and $1.01. The Mormon Outposts overall have managed well, with an increase of only 55 cents a gallon from last year. . . .

But there are some differences in what gas actually costs today because there are differences in what those communities usually pay. So, on average, gas in less-wealthy Minority Central counties is 20 cents-a-gallon cheaper than it is in the Monied Burbs. And the people who live in and around the nation's biggest cities—the Industrial Metropolis counties—pay the most of all.

Understanding the pain, however, is not that simple, because in the end what you pay for gas is only a part (sometimes a small part) of your actual gas bill and of rising prices. Among other things, taxes play a role, as well as the formula blends required in your area.

There are also bigger questions about what kind of car you drive and how long your commute is. No one likes $4-a-gallon gas, but it helps if you only have to fill up every other week, or even live car-less, as you might be more likely to do in a dense urban area.

And, of course, there is how much disposable income you have. Are you diverting money into your gas tank that was supposed to be going to your family vacation to London or that was supposed to be going to your grocery bill? That makes a difference in what the gas price hike means.

Where It Hurts . . . and for How Long

Look at the higher prices in the small town Service Worker Centers and the African-American heavy Minority Central counties, where gas prices are up 94 cents-a-gallon and 93 cents-a-gallon respectively in the last year.

[The] increase in gas prices . . . is going to eat away at the thing the U.S. economy needs to get going again— consumer spending.

In both those county types, the unemployment rate is still over 10 percent. People there . . . , on average, were hit hard by the recession as we have noted in other reporting and are still in pretty bad straits. When they have to basically pay an extra dollar for every gallon of gas the headwinds for them get stronger. The pain in those places is felt directly and pushes any recovery talk off.

Add in the fact that they are more rural locales, places where driving tends to be more necessary, and you compound the problem. Kip Ward, who lives in Lincoln City, Ore., a Service Worker Center that Patchwork Nation visits, figures his daily commute, home and back, at 400–500 miles a week.

The Monied Burbs have bounced back some from the recession, but increase in gas prices there is going to eat away at the thing the U.S. economy needs to get going again—consumer spending. Most of the people who live in these counties aren't poor, but pulling an extra $50 a week away from them will make an impact. That's money that can't be spent at local coffee shops and restaurants.

And, yes, higher gas prices will take a toll on family vacations in the Monied Burbs, many of which are taken in tourist hubs like, Lincoln City and other Service Worker Centers.

Tractor Country counties, rural and not especially wealthy, rely on fuel not only for driving, but also for farming equipment. They would seem to be especially hard hit, but the agricultural economy in them shielded them from most of the great recession and rising food costs actually have helped them.

"At $7 a bushel for corn, they better not complain about anything," joked Dennis Walstra, Mayor of Sioux Center, Iowa, a Tractor Country community we visit. That was a few weeks back. Corn is now at $7.60 a bushel.

2012 Approaches

There is no sign as yet that the gas price increase is over. In fact, further political instability in the Middle East, could push it higher still—closer to $5 or more.

And, while it is early, all of this could end up being a big part of the coming presidential race. Much of your economic reality is perception. Whatever the national headlines say about the stock market or the job market, it's what you see and feel outside your door that makes the real impact.

The potential for a prolonged, painful recovery can't be welcome news at the White House. Even if gas prices have returned to earth by then, the impacts on the economy and the recovery will likely linger. The 2012 political field has not yet taken shape, but the economic landscape may be starting to and so far it is not pretty.

Rising Gas Prices Transfer Wealth from Poorer Americans to the Rich

Dan Froomkin

Dan Froomkin is senior Washington correspondent for The Huffington Post, *a web-based American newspaper and blog.*

The next time you're gritting your teeth as you fill your tank with $4 gas, here's something to consider: Your pain is their gain.

The last of the Big Five oil companies announced first-quarter earnings Friday, so the totals are in. Between the five of them, ExxonMobil, BP, Shell, Chevron, and ConocoPhillips made $34 billion in profits in the first three months of 2011—up 42 percent from a year ago.

That's about $110 for every man, woman, and child in the United States—in just three months.

Exxon alone cleared a cool $10.7 billion profit from January through March, up 69 percent from 2010. That's $82,175 a minute.

Enriching the Rich

Why the staggering increase in earnings? Precisely because you're paying $4 a gallon for gas.

Gas prices shoot up when oil prices shoot up, and when oil prices shoot up for reasons that have nothing to do with how much it costs to bring it out of the ground, it's a windfall for the folks who produce it.

The average cost to produce a barrel of oil, including exploration, development, extraction and taxes, is about $30, according to a U.S. Energy Information Administration survey. The going rate to buy one is about $113.

Why is the price so high? Part of it is increased demand and geopolitical worries. But no less an authority on the matter than Goldman Sachs acknowledged earlier this month [April 2011] that speculation is at least partially responsible, driving oil prices up faster and higher than supply and demand could possibly explain.

That means the people who are betting on oil prices are actually making the price of oil go up.

And while the pain is widely felt—consider all the Wal-Mart shoppers who are agonizing over how to make it to the end of the month—the benefits are not being widely shared.

The industry's powerful Washington mouthpiece, the American Petroleum Institute, argues that the staggering earnings simply reflect oil and gas companies' tremendous contributions to the economy, and that their stock prices are shoring up the nation's pension funds.

Every visit to the gas pump reflects a transfer of money from the many to the few—and in most cases, from the not-so-rich to the super-rich.

Adam Sieminski, chief energy economist for Deutsche Bank, thinks the numbers get too much attention. "The overall profit numbers look really big because they're really big companies that move a lot of product around," he says. "To say that they're enormous profits only works if you're talking about the total number. They're not enormous profits if you compare them across other companies and other industries."

Siemenski even accentuates the positive. "Yes, when gas goes up, everybody squeaks, because it's uncomfortable," he says. But high oil prices mean, among other things, that "it becomes more attractive to do alternative energy. . . . The worst thing that ever happened to wind and solar power companies was when oil prices collapsed in 2008 and early 2009," he says. Furthermore, when gas gets pricey, "people who made a decision to get a Prius instead of a Hummer get a payback, and from a societal standpoint, that's probably good."

And yet, the fact of the matter is that every visit to the gas pump reflects a transfer of money from the many to the few—and in most cases, from the not-so-rich to the super-rich.

Enriching Shareholders

By and large, the oil companies' profits are not finding their way back into the communities from which they came; are not being used to create more jobs; and are not being invested in new equipment and exploration.

Some of that money is going back out the door in the form of larger dividends to stockholders. But in the case of two of the big five in particular—Exxon and ConocoPhillips—more than half of their total profits are being used to buy back their own stock.

Fully $5.7 billion of Exxon's haul went to buy back its own stock—and the company announced that it expects to buy back yet another $5 billion's worth in the second quarter of the year. Conoco earned $3 billion in the first three months of 2011—and spent $1.6 billion of that to buy back 21 million of its own shares.

Buying back stock is not an uncommon tactic among publicly held companies, particularly when they experience a sudden and possibly temporary uptick in revenue. Buybacks are almost guaranteed to send stock prices up, by boosting earnings per outstanding share, increasing the demand for the stock and sending a signal that the company thinks its stock is undervalued.

But from the viewpoint of a company's CEO, other top brass and its board of directors, stock buybacks have all sorts of particular advantages, as well.

Top executives, after all, often get significant stock options. If stock prices don't go up, such options are worthless. By contrast, the higher the stock price goes, the more valuable the option. (Exxon's stock is up 32 percent from six months ago.)

Buying back shares benefits existing shareholders, no one else. And more than anyone else, it benefits existing management.

Companies that buy back their stock can either retire it or simply keep it themselves, under the control of the board of directors, to reissue later or award as bonuses.

Dividends, by contrast, are not nearly as good a deal for company executives. For one thing, they are taxed as income. An increase in the stock price is not taxed as income; it's not taxed at all until the stock is sold—and only then at the capital gains tax rate, which is limited to 15 percent. (Fifteen percent would be a lot for the median American family, which pays less than 5 percent of its income in federal taxes. But it's a huge break to those paying income tax at the highest marginal rate of 35 percent.)

"Buying back shares benefits existing shareholders, no one else. And more than anyone else, it benefits existing management," says Henry Banta, an energy industry analyst and partner in the Washington D.C. law firm of Lobel, Novins & Lamont.

"They're basically enriching themselves," says Daniel J. Weiss, a senior fellow at the Center for American Progress. "With this windfall, they enrich the board of directors, senior managers, and shareholders."

And in 2007, when Exxon was using $30 billion a year from the previous oil-price bubble to buy back its shares, *Bloomberg* columnist David Pauly wrote: "In most cases, stock buybacks are suspect. . . . Managements should ignore investors' call to repurchase their shares and invest money in ways that will increase profit, not just earnings per share."

Most Shareholders Already Are Rich

As for the dividends paid by Exxon and the other oil giants, there may be a lot of shareholders, total—including a lot of pension funds and mutual funds—but the vast majority of shares are held by a very small elite.

Edward N. Wolff, an economics professor at New York University, studies wealth distribution. His latest study includes data through 2007. When it comes to total equity in stocks, Wolff says, "it's still very concentrated in the hands of the rich."

"Less than half of households owned stock as of 2007," he says. "Probably less now" because of the financial crisis, he suspects: "Probably more like 45 percent, maybe less." That includes 401ks, mutual funds and the like.

"Even that really overstates things because a lot of the people who do own stock own very small amounts," Wolff says. As of 2007, the percentage of households that owned $5,000 or more of stock was 35 percent; only 22 percent owned $25,000 or more.

Who's got the rest? The wealthiest 1 percent of households has 38 percent, Wolff found; the wealthiest 5 percent has 69 percent; the wealthiest 10 percent has 81 percent.

The bottom 60 percent of households owns 2.5 percent of the total stock. Not so very much.

Hoarding Profits

There's another thing the big oil companies are doing with their profits: they're hoarding them. If precedent holds, as soon as oil prices started shooting up again, a lot of that money started going into the bank for safekeeping—and adding yet more to the $1 trillion or so in corporate cash lying fallow and slowing the recovery.

And as it happens, a not insubstantial chunk of last quarter's profits were a direct gift—from the taxpayers. Somewhere between $4 billion and $9 billion of the industry's annual profits comes from federal subsidies.

President Barack Obama has proposed repealing $4 billion a year in subsidies; the American Petroleum Institute says the proposal would actually cost the industry about $90 billion over the next decade.

Response to Obama's proposal was lackluster at first, from both sides of the aisle.

But Democrats, afraid of being thrown out of the White House by an angry, gas-impoverished voting public, are suddenly seeing the fight to repeal those subsidies as a winning political issue.

Although the repeal would neither increase nor decrease the price of gas, it would take a bite out of Big Oil. And pushing for the repeal will almost inevitably highlight the modern Republican Party's nearly lockstep allegiance to the thriving oil and gas interests—something that, in a period of high gas prices and even higher profits, couldn't be good for them.

But yet another thing the industry does with all its cash is buy influence in Washington.

For instance, Exxon, during the same quarter it made nearly $11 billion, spent just a tiny fraction of that on lobbying. But that was still a whopping $3 million.

High Gas Prices Are Causing Many Americans Financial Hardship

Lydia Saad

Lydia Saad is a senior editor at Gallup, a public opinion survey firm.

The slight majority of Americans, 53%, say they have responded to today's steep gas prices by making major changes in their personal lives, while 46% say they have not. Sizable proportions of adults of all major income levels have made such changes, including 68% of low-income Americans, 54% of middle-income Americans, and 44% of upper-income Americans. . . .

Although employed Americans are more likely to report driving an above-average amount—and are thus greater consumers of gasoline—they are less likely than non-employed Americans to have made major lifestyle changes to deal with rising gas prices, 49% vs. 58%. This likely reflects the higher average income of employed Americans, but may also indicate they have less flexibility in their lives to cut back on driving.

These findings come from a *USA Today*/Gallup poll conducted May 12–15 [2011], in which 67% of Americans say the recent high gas prices have caused them financial hardship, including 21% who say they have caused them severe hardship. This is among the highest levels of reported hardship Gallup has seen on this measure since 2000, and is similar to the 71% found when average gas prices nationwide topped $4 per gallon in 2008 and the 72% when they first exceeded $3 per gallon in 2005. . . .

Americans Driving Less, Steering Toward Cars That Are More Fuel Efficient

Among the 53% of Americans who report having made major changes in their lives to deal with gas prices, the most common strategy, mentioned by a third of them, is simply driving less. Additionally, 16% specifically report they are cutting back on vacation travel, 15% are being more careful in planning errands and other local trips, and 15% have either purchased a more fuel-efficient vehicle or are looking into it. Smaller segments are doing less "leisure driving," carpooling, using public transportation, walking more, biking more, and driving more slowly.

While equal percentages of men and women say they are driving less in response to changes in gas prices, men are nearly twice as likely as women to say they have purchased or plan to purchase a more fuel-efficient car.

Rather than driving less, 12% of those making major changes due to gas prices say they are cutting back on groceries, clothes, and other expenses to absorb the higher gas costs. . . .

Low-income Americans who have made major lifestyle changes due to high gas prices primarily report significant hardships, including driving less and cutting back on household expenses. By contrast, those in middle- and upper-income households are relatively more likely to report driving less for vacations and errands.

Additionally, while equal percentages of men and women say they are driving less in response to changes in gas prices, men are nearly twice as likely as women to say they have purchased or plan to purchase a more fuel-efficient car, 20% vs. 11%. Women, on the other hand, are twice as likely (16% vs. 8%) to say they have cut back on other household expenses.

The responses of adults who have made changes to deal with high gas prices vary by age, with those 55 and older much more likely than younger adults to say they have been more careful about running errands but less likely to say they are using a more fuel-efficient car.

Bottom Line

Average gas prices in the United States have increased by nearly $1 a gallon since January [2011], with half of that increase occurring since March. This increase has clearly caught Americans' attention, with 67% saying it has caused them financial hardship. Additionally, the slight majority of Americans report that they have made real changes in their lives to deal with high fuel costs. Driving less is the obvious, and most common, response, whether that be driving less in general, cutting back on vacation travel, or consolidating errands. Additionally, some Americans, particularly those under 55, have switched to a more fuel-efficient car, while others, particularly lower-income Americans, have cut back on other household and living expenses to be able to put gas in their tanks.

Compared with Other Industrialized Countries, US Gas Is Cheap

Sarah Terry-Cobo

Sarah Terry-Cobo, formerly a reporter and research assistant on the Center for Investigative Reporting's Carbon Watch series, is a freelance reporter specializing in science and environmental policy issues.

What's the true price of gasoline? . . . California has some of the dirtiest air in the nation. Consequently, it has some of the strictest rules for gasoline, meaning it burns cleaner than it does in many other states. But cleaner fuels are more expensive.

Clean air requirements, combined with supply and refining constraints, make the price of California gas consistently among the highest in the nation. Turmoil in the Middle East is another factor that pushes up the global price of crude oil. Even though the average price for a gallon of regular unleaded gas in California fluctuates around $4, some experts argue that $4 a gallon is much less than the real cost.

Compared with other industrialized countries, the U.S. has it cheap. *The Economist* notes that American consumers pay about half of what Europeans pay, which is up to about $8.50 per gallon (or $2.25 per liter). The media website Good has a nifty chart showing the disparity in prices across the Atlantic, and PBS' *NewsHour* explains the effect Middle East turmoil has on the retail price of gas. While politicians on both sides of the aisle bicker about why gas is expensive, Sen. Jeff Bingaman, (D-N.M.), is one who explains the real reasons, and as David Roberts notes, he is lonely in doing so.

The Cost of Clean Air

Even though reducing toxic chemicals in gasoline might make it more expensive, the EPA [Environmental Protection Agency] argues that clean air provides long-term cost benefits. A recent study of the Clean Air Act showed "the public health and environmental benefits . . . exceed their costs by a margin of four to one."

From 1990 to 2010, these regulations have prevented "23,000 Americans from dying prematurely, [and] averted over 1,700,000 incidences of asthma attacks and aggravation of chronic asthma." In the same two decades, it also prevented more than 4.1 million lost workdays due to pollution-related illnesses.

California is among the leaders in the U.S. in implementing clean-air regulations to limit pollution from carbon dioxide and other greenhouse gases. Its ambitious Global Warming Solutions Act aims to reduce greenhouse-gas pollution to 1990 levels by the year 2020—goals similar to the United Nations' Kyoto Protocol. And the state's Air Resources Board will introduce the nation's second pollution-trading system, known as cap-and-trade, for greenhouse gases on Jan. 1, 2012. Under that system, if a company does not meet its pollution limits, it can buy a carbon offset, a promise to reduce pollution elsewhere.

But the market isn't the only method the board is using to reduce air pollution and greenhouse gases. In fact, the board estimates only one-fifth of the reductions will come from cap-and-trade. The other four-fifths will come from increased energy-efficiency standards, improved recycling and composting programs, the highest standard for fuel efficiency in cars, and the state's low-carbon fuel standard.

The cost of clean air programs may be high, but so is the cost of pollution. A 2008 study commissioned by CSU [California State University] Fullerton's Institute for Economic and Environmental Studies notes that the cost of air pollution for the greater Los Angeles region adds up to more than $1,250 per person per year.

For the Central Valley, where one-third of the nation's produce originates, the cost is more than $1,600 per person per year. These costs include treatment for respiratory illnesses like asthma, which are disproportionately borne by children younger than 5, the elderly, and minority populations. Other costs include lost workdays, missed school days, and premature deaths.

But health effects are just some of the financial impacts of burning fossil fuels—gasoline and diesel fuel, in particular. Harmful air pollution can affect food and fiber crops. The U.S. Global Change Research Program noted in a 2009 report on climate change that greenhouse gases can reduce crop yields for "soybeans, wheat, oats, green beans, peppers, and some types of cotton."

Although $4 a gallon may seem expensive, there are many social and environmental costs that Americans don't pay for at the pump.

And the cost of oil spills? Some early estimates put the price of cleaning up the massive spill in the Gulf of Mexico at up to $20 billion. Every year, states spend more than $600 million to clean up leaking underground gasoline storage tanks.

In the last three decades, businesses, states, and the EPA have cleaned up 401,874 leaking underground gasoline storage tanks, with an estimated 93,123 more sites awaiting cleanup, according to an EPA representative. In 2010, the agency set aside $66.2 million in a fund for states to use for cleanup activities. The agency spends about $2 million to $3 million each year for cleanup on tribal land.

Although $4 a gallon may seem expensive, there are many social and environmental costs that Americans don't pay for at the pump. While these costs are hidden, the cost to society is high.

This story was produced by the Center for Investigative Reporting, the nation's oldest independent, nonprofit investigative news center in the United States. More at cironline.org.

High Gas Prices Might Shock the Nation into Cutting Its Dependence on Oil

Myles Spicer

Myles Spicer is an author, writer, and blogger who frequently blogs for Daily Kos, *a progressive online news site and weblog with political analysis on US current events.*

Recently, there has been a blizzard of editorials about the need for conservation of oil and gas. While I heartily agree with this position, I fear the American public is merely tilting at windmills. Why? Because all these sermons about energy conservation lack both urgency and reality. And that is dangerously unacceptable.

There is absolutely nothing new in what you are going to read here—and that is exactly why it is so interesting.

There is no gas "crisis" that has suddenly appeared. There are no "surprises" to $4/gallon gas. Everything—everything—that has precipitated this rise in price has been known for at least decades. So why is there so much shock and discussion?

Consider these facts:

- First and foremost, oil is a finite product! It was never if we were going to run out of oil . . . it was always when. The real problem is that no one ever seems to address that issue, as long as oil remains cheap. Gutless leaders avoided telling us that; the oil companies and automakers stonewall it; and consequently, Americans just don't get it! And of course now [in January 2008], the leadership of our country is in the hands of two former oil company executives—both of whom lead us to believe we can "drill our way" out of this situation. That may be good for their compatriots in the oil industry, but it is no solution to this problem. In fact, it is counter-productive in a variety of ways.

- The major portion of world oil production has always been in the hands of despotic, uncaring, unreliable countries. Nothing new here.

- Americans have enjoyed the very lowest gas prices (and gas taxes) for decades; and we have known that forever.

- The oil companies are cleaning up in this apparently "new" crisis . . . and cleaning our pockets as well. We know that, too. Exxon made $15 billion of net profit in the past . . . 6 month[s] alone. . . . Surprised? You shouldn't be—it's easily discovered from many financial sources. If, as [former] President [George W.] Bush says, we are in a "war", then I have always believed profiteering during a war bordered on immoral, if not illegal.

- Natural disasters, such as [Hurricane] Katrina, are common, almost annual occurrences around the world, which periodically impede oil production. This is not new.

- The Energy Bill earlier passed by the Republican Congress had strong incentives for more drilling . . . and meager incentives for alternate energy, and limited emphasis on conservation. Again, crafted with the direction of the Bush team, it provided significant additional handouts to the oil companies, which is exactly what we do not need. The bill was widely reported—no surprises here either. The only possible surprise, to me, is the lack of outrage.

- Mass transit in our country is decades behind in development. The busses have a reputation for low class travel; the trains are woefully behind Europe and Asia; and local mass transit is far behind as well. But we know that.

The Need for $10/Gallon Gasoline

So, if we know all this; and if it is not new; and if it will eventually have grave consequences, then why is nothing being done? And, why would I propose $10/gallon gasoline? Well, the second question answers the first. We just do not get it!

Incremental raises just pinch, but do not really hurt. The oil cartel is very clever about this—they keep price points high enough to gobble up unconscionable amounts of money, but low enough so we are not incented to seek alternatives. We continue to buy our SUVs, we burn fossil fuels like there is no tomorrow, and we complain. Under this system, no leader has emerged to tell us the Emperor has no clothes. Alternate energy sources continue to lag. And there is no really effective solution in sight. Worse yet, there is absolutely no urgency to this very critical and imminent issue. If you think $100/barrel oil is expensive now, consider what the last barrel removed from the earth will be worth. In fact, that barrel will likely end up in the Smithsonian as a relic of a past civilization. Hopefully there will be some sort of transit available to go see it!

The only real solution [to oil dependency] is a shock so enormous and devastating that it will . . . wake us up to the reality of the situation.

Regarding alternate energy sources, I have for years examined the stock in a variety of Hydrogen, wind power and other alternate energy companies. I like to track these efforts. Without exception, these firms are small, under funded, losing money (few if any are profitable), and very much on the fringe of our economy. Plus, there is little coordination among them to synergize their efforts. Take Hydrogen for example. Yes, we can produce Hydrogen-powered vehicles, but the mass production for fuel, distribution, storage and other requirements to make it a viable fuel are decades away. The race to find a replacement for oil-based fuels, as well as the abundance of that resource, may already be lost.

> *The only real solution [to oil dependency] is a shock so enormous and devastating that it will . . . wake us up to the reality of the situation.*

And when will that be? I am not an oil expert, all we DO know is that there is only so much of it on earth . . . we are burning it by the billions of barrels each year . . . less is being discovered and all is harder to get . . . the emerging nations are coming online to exacerbate consumption . . . the world's population is growing quickly . . . and it will run out. In 15 years? In 30 years? Even 40 years? What does it matter? At best it is a generation or two. Curiously, Saudi Arabia, which supplies 1/8 of the world's production is quite secretive and unclear about its true remaining reserves. And more drilling only prolongs the demise of fossil fuels, and keeps us asleep. That is the real danger of drilling in the Alaskan Wildlife Preserve [Arctic National Wildlife Preserve]—it is not a solution. In my mind, the only real solution is a shock so enormous and devastating that it will once and for all wake us up to the reality of the situation. At $10/gallon, that would get someone's attention.

Maybe we could get a leader who tells us the truth of the situation, creates a national (or even international) full court press on alternate energy sources, and levies an excess profits tax on the oil companies. Especially one not wedded to the oil industry.

Maybe we can finally get people off the roads and onto a clean, fast, widely scaled mass transit system that will be built in years, not decades. Maybe Americans will discover the pleasures of travel in speedy, beautiful trains with first class service and downtown to downtown service. Maybe, for regional travel, busses will become cleaner and more attractive; and terminals will be located in desirable parts of towns.

But, none of this will happen with small incremental raises in the cost of gas; and there is the added problem that these small increases hurt the poor more than any others—especially the working poor who must travel to jobs. At $10/gallon, the outrage of the average worker would be so great and disasterous, action would be demanded—not just complaining. So, maybe rather than slowly bleeding to death, we might be better "getting it on" and get our wake up call sooner than later.

So, what will it take? $10/gallon gasoline would surely do it. But there is one other solution that is even better. . . . That is $3/gallon gas . . . and the hope that America finally wakes up, elects some gutsy leadership, and does all that is needed NOW to assure our continuing prosperity. Hello . . . is anyone listening?

There Are Many Benefits to Higher Gas Prices

KNS Financial

KNS Financial, a personal financial advice company, was founded by New Jersey economist Khaleef Crumbley. Crumbley, using his company name, has written numerous articles for Redeeming Riche$, a financial blog and website.

In the last few months [early 2011] we have seen a sharp increase in the price of oil. This has caused many to search for ways to save money on gas—from driving less to finding cheaper gas! However, higher energy prices are not a universally negative situation, and there are some who actually welcome the increase due to the many benefits of higher gas prices. . . .

Changes in Consumer Behavior

Most of us simply drive along to and from work, church, grocery stores, events, friends' homes, and anywhere else that we feel like going. It isn't until gas prices begin to skyrocket that we began to consider our actions. As with pretty much every other good or service, higher prices leads to lower demand.

Whenever we see a rapid surge in gas prices, we tend to see a lot more people carpooling (even posting ads on Craigslist); the sale of fuel-efficient vehicles rise, and people even consider public transportation. Some even begin to wonder if their car is a luxury or necessity!

Employers even start to offer telecommuting (working from home) as a perk to many employees—or as a way to show employee appreciation.

Also, when more of our income is devoted to gas and energy costs, we tend to cut back on more frivolous activities. This sudden burst of financial responsibility can definitely be seen as one of the benefits of higher gas prices!

New Technology Seems More Affordable

There are alternative sources of energy available to us today. However, they typically are more expensive to produce and access than oil. This means that when oil/gas prices are cheap, no one gives a second thought to these other sources of energy. However, once oil prices begin to soar, it becomes much easier for proponents of alternative energy sources (and their respective industries) to be taken seriously.

This goes for alternative energy sources, such as solar power for houses and corporate buildings, wind and hydroelectric power for small communities, and even electric hybrid vehicles. Also, we must consider research and development of alternative fuel sources—such as ethanol from sugar cane or corn—as another benefit of higher gas prices.

This doesn't even take into consideration all of the oil that is used to make various plastics, medicine, clothing, and fertilizer! When the price of oil rises, research into alternative inputs for the manufacturing of these items increases along with it!

Certain Industries Will Take Off

Many industries hate seeing higher oil prices, as it makes their cost of doing business that much higher. It gets more expensive to make certain materials, ship intermediate and finished goods, travel to meetings, and many other aspects of business. Workers begin to demand more money in order to offset their own increased cost of living as well.

However, there are some industries that thrive when oil prices shoot up! With more expensive oil, you will have an increased interest in surveying, drilling and extracting, transporting, and refining the costly energy source!

Not only will these companies and their suppliers see good times, but higher prices should mean a lot more jobs are created within these sectors as well! Another group that benefits from higher gas prices are the shareholders in these various companies.

Higher Tax Revenue

In thinking of the benefits of higher gas prices, we can't forget our dear old uncle Sam. Every time a gallon of gas is sold, a portion of that price goes to our government in the form of taxes. The more that is collected in the form of gasoline tax, the less tax help is needed from other areas!

CHAPTER 3

Is Public Transportation an Answer to Rising Gasoline Prices?

Chapter Preface

O ne of the most controversial public transportation issues in the United States is whether it makes sense to build high-speed rail systems similar to those in other countries, such as France, Spain, Germany, and China. Although several states have rejected such proposals, California voters in 2008 passed a proposition authorizing $9.95 billion in general obligation bonds to finance a high-speed rail system. The California system, as planned, would eventually link all major California cities, including San Diego, Los Angeles, San Jose, Fresno, San Francisco, and Sacramento—eight hundred miles of track with a total of twenty-four different stations. If built, high-speed trains will travel on this system at about 220 miles per hour, allowing passengers to travel between major metropolitan regions of Los Angeles and San Francisco in under three hours, and all the way from San Diego to Sacramento in a little more than three-and-a-half hours. The costs of building such a system, however, are huge, especially at a time when the nation is focused on budget cuts and the national debt. This and other criticisms may ultimately doom the California high-speed rail project before it ever gets started.

According to its proponents, high-speed rail has a number of advantages and benefits, not the least of which is that it would be an important, high-tech infrastructure upgrade for America, allowing Americans to take pride in the nation's ability to still think big. In addition, the California High-Speed Rail Authority (CHSRA), an agency created to develop and shepherd the project through to completion, says high-speed rail would produce real economic, environmental, and community benefits. Perhaps most importantly, the project would create many new jobs, not only to build the rail system but also to staff and maintain it. Also, cities served by the high-speed train system are expected to see expansive economic development around the new rail stations, as local transportation is connected to the rail terminals and restaurants and other businesses are created to service rail passengers. And California businesses are expected to benefit generally from quicker transportation of people and goods, and relief of congestion on nearby freeways. In addition, supporters claim that high-speed rail will turn a profit, unlike slower train systems that are notorious for slow and poor service. The environment will benefit, meanwhile, because trains will run on electric power that will increasingly be obtained from renewable energy sources such as wind and solar, reducing air pollution and smog. And these fast trains use only a fraction of the energy used by planes or cars, so that will reduce gasoline usage as well as greenhouse gas emissions.

High-speed rail detractors, on the other hand, generally emphasize the high cost of building such elaborate rail systems. One group critical of the California plan, Californians Advocating Responsible Rail Design, has estimated that the total cost of the California high-speed rail project will be $65 billion, and others have speculated that this could rise to $100 billion with inflation over the years it will take to build. In fact, original cost estimates have already proven to be low. The initial San Francisco-to-Anaheim segment was initially estimated by the CHSRA to cost between $35.7 and $42.6 billion, but a more recent estimate was $63 billion.

Much of this money will have to come from federal funds, with the rest supplied by the state. However, the US Congress is in a budget-cutting mood, especially with regard to public transit monies, so the prospects of cuts in federal funding loom. In September 2011, for example, the House of Representatives' Appropriation Subcommittee on Transportation, Housing and Urban Development reduced President Barack Obama's fiscal 2012 request for $8 billion for rail systems to $7 billion, cutting funds for California's project and funding only Amtrak and some smaller rail programs. This legislation still must be approved by the Appropriations Committee, and both the full House and the Senate, but it threatens to halt California's high-speed rail dream. CHSRA can use about $6.3 billion in earlier federal grants and monies from an initial bond offering that state taxpayers approved in 2008, but these sources would pay for only a part of the initial rail segment. California Governor Jerry Brown has decided to review the entire project before agreeing to issue additional state bonds, and some commentators suggest that the state must secure private funding to make the project possible.

Yet the potential for private funding depends on just how profitable high-speed rail might be once it is built. According to supporters, the one US high-speed rail system currently in place—Amtrak's Acela Express service linking Washington, DC, with Boston—is profitable, even though Amtrak as a whole is not. But most of the other high-speed rail systems in the world, such as those in Europe, are government-subsidized. According to some estimates, Germany's system is one of the most expensive, requiring annual subsidies of $11.6 billion over ten years ending in 2006. Some commentators say it may be possible to cover operating costs from rider fees, but probably not capital costs such as maintenance and replacement parts.

Other obstacles facing California's high-speed rail development are the objections from property owners who will live close to planned rail routes. Already, angry citizens from the communities of Atherton, Palo Alto, and Menlo Park have begun protesting the project, after realizing that it could mean constructing elevated train tracks through the middle of town—construction that Palo Alto residents have said would divide the city like a Berlin wall. Opposition has only increased as planning for the project has continued. Because of this opposition, and because the $6.3 billion in federal funds must be spent before 2012, the state has decided it must start the project in the Central Valley, rather than in the more populated San Francisco corridor—a decision that could result in a railroad to nowhere if the rest of the rail line is never built.

High-speed rail is the most ambitious type of public transportation project being considered, but many public transportation advocates would rather see government funds spent on maintaining and upgrading existing means of public transit, such as buses and subways. Viewpoints in this chapter examine whether various types of mass transit might offer alternatives to cars in this age of rising gas prices.

Rising Gas Prices in 2011 Caused Drivers to Turn to Public Transportation

Sean Barry

Sean Barry is a campaign associate for Transportation for America, a coalition of housing, business, environmental, public health, transportation, equitable development, and other organizations dedicated to improving America's transportation system.

The higher gas prices become, the more likely people are to start looking for alternatives. And the shift has already begun.

Demand for mass transit is surging everywhere—from Nashville, Tennessee to Eau Claire, Wisconsin; Terre Haute, Indiana to Pasadena, California. Virginia Governor Bob McDonnell is encouraging his constituents to bike, walk or carpool at least once every two weeks. And, residents in Peoria and central Illinois started coordinating ridesharing schedules online.

In that same vein, the *Las Cruces Sun-News*, one of the largest newspapers in New Mexico, encouraged readers to consider new options in an editorial this week [April 2011] opining:

> The economic decision to choose public transportation over one's personal vehicle could turn into a positive for all concerned.
>
> People who've never tried it may actually like it. And if a bus is going where they're going? Yes, they'll be more likely

to continue using that mode of transportation. It beats paying almost $4 a gallon for gasoline, especially when the personal vehicle gets about 15 miles per almost $4.

Last time gas prices topped $4 and demand for [public] transit surged, . . . some of the biggest increases in demand came in areas less associated with transit, like the Southwest.

Rising Demand for Public Transportation

Gas prices at or above $4 a gallon generate the need for 670 million additional passenger trips on transit systems, resulting in more than 10.8 billion trips per year, according to the American Public Transportation Association.

Bicycling has become a popular alternative, with new riders benefiting from recent investment in bike facilities and programs. Mirroring the increased demand for transit in 2008, biking increased 15 percent nationwide and 23 percent in the 31 largest bike-friendly cities that year, with a similar uptick occurring today, according to Peopleforbikes.org.

Last time gas prices topped $4 and demand for transit surged, cities with well-established public transit systems like New York and Boston saw increases in transit usage of 5 percent of more, while some of the biggest increases in demand came in areas less associated with transit, like the Southwest. But these are many of the same communities that lack the capacity for a large surge in ridership.

Often lost in the discussion is the fact that many people are stuck without realistic alternatives to pain at the pump: streets too dangerous to walk or bike, destinations too far away, no available transit service, no easy options.

Most of the talk in Washington has focused on the supply side of the gas prices equation—speculation, domestic drilling and the like. But a real-world shift in demand is happening right before our eyes. With the nation's comprehensive surface transportation bill overdue for renewal, this ought to lend greater urgency to the need for robust investment in an array of options to ensure no one gets stranded or left behind.

Record Mass Transit Ridership Could Result If Gas Prices Rise Higher

PR Newswire

PR Newswire is a global provider of news and information distribution services for public relations professionals and other communicators.

A study released today [March 2011] by the American Public Transportation Association (APTA) predicts that as gasoline prices continue increasing, Americans will turn to public transportation in record numbers. APTA is calling on Congress to address this impending demand by providing a greater long-term investment in public transportation.

Public Transit Ridership Increases

The analysis reveals if regular gas prices reach $4 a gallon across the nation, as many experts have forecasted, an additional 670 million passenger trips could be expected, resulting in more than 10.8 billion trips per year. If pump prices jump to $5 a gallon, the report predicts an additional 1.5 billion passenger trips can be expected, resulting in more than 11.6 billion trips per year. And if prices were to soar to $6 a gallon, expectations go as high as an additional 2.7 billion passenger trips, resulting in more than 12.9 billion trips per year.

"The volatility of the price at the pump is another wake up call for our nation to address the increasing demand for public transportation services," said APTA President William Millar. "We must make significant, long-term investments in public transportation or we will leave our fellow Americans with limited travel options, or in many cases stranded without travel options. Public transit is the quickest way for people to beat high gas prices if it is available."

The [Barack] Obama Administration's transportation authorization blueprint and proposal ... increases public transit investment by 128 percent over the next six years.

Many of the public transit systems across the country are already seeing large ridership increases, some reaching double digits in the month of February as compared to the previous year. For instance; the South Florida Regional Transportation Authority in Pompano Beach, FL increased by 10.6 percent; Southeastern Pennsylvania Transportation Authority of Philadelphia, PA increased by 10 percent; and the Capitol Corridor Joint Powers Authority of Oakland, CA increased by 14 percent.

"We saw this same story in 2008 and several times before where high gas prices caught our country without adequate travel options," said Millar. "However, this time we can write a happy ending and make sure investment is made to expand public transportation so that more Americans have a choice in how they travel."

Public Transit Investments Needed

APTA supports the [Barack] Obama Administration's transportation authorization blueprint and proposal which increases public transit investment by 128 percent over the next six years. This type of investment would help close the gap for the 46 percent of Americans who do not have access to public transportation. . . .

The projected estimates use the 2010 APTA Public Transportation Ridership Report as a baseline. The ridership is then increased by the reported elasticity multiplied by the projected price change to show ridership growth at a given increase above the average price for regular gasoline as reported in the last 2010 report by the Energy Information Administration of the U.S. Department of Energy.

The United States Must Invest in Public Transportation

Christian Science Monitor

The Christian Science Monitor *provides national and international news both online and through its weekly news magazine.*

High gas prices are prying record numbers of Americans from their cars and onto buses, subways, and commuter trains. That has many pluses: It eases pocketbook expenses, road congestion, and pollution. But it's also straining providers of mass transit—a signal for needed change.

In Washington DC, the Metro subway and bus system is so stretched at peak hours that officials say the government and other large employers may have to mandate staggered work schedules if gas goes over $5 a gallon—once unimaginable.

In San Francisco and the Bay Area, seats near the doors of some BART trains have been removed to create more standing room for a surge in commuters. Meanwhile, about 20 percent of the nation's public bus operators have had to reduce service because of the high cost of diesel fuel, according to the American Public Transport Association (APTA).

Expanding Mass Transit—A Difficult Task

Mass-transit ridership that's at its highest in 50 years presents an opportunity to beef up outdated systems in many areas of the country. But it's not going to be easy.

For starters, the same price pinch that's squeezing drivers is being felt by transit operators. They must pay more for fuel and their revenue sources are declining as the economy slows.

More people may be exchanging traffic for tokens, but in some cases, fares cover as little as 20 percent of operating expenses. Mass transit depends greatly on local, state, and federal money—from sales taxes, for instance, which are slowing with the economy, and from gas taxes, which have not kept up with inflation.

Only 20 percent of Americans live near public transport.

As a result, public transit operators are increasing fares and delaying projects and improvements—just what the country doesn't need at a time of increased demand. APTA estimates that $45 billion to $60 billion annually is what's needed to invest in America's aging public buses, rail transit, and facilities. Yet current capital spending is only about $13 billion a year.

Public officials may wonder whether the demand is here to stay. During the 1970s oil crises, when folks lined up for gas, public ridership increased—but then dropped again. Only 5 percent of Americans now commute to work using public transport.

America's passion for automobiles—for the independence and comfort they provide—runs deep, and carmakers want to keep it that way with more fuel-efficient models. At the same time, only 20 percent of Americans live near public transport.

It's one thing to take temporary measures such as extending hours, adding more train cars, and bringing back bus-only lanes. It's quite another to expand train station parking areas and construct subway or light rail lines.

But those who hesitate should consider this: The days of $1.50-a-gallon gas are long gone, while traffic congestion is growing. Over the next 50 years, the US population is expected to increase by 150 million people. An ongoing trend back to urban areas shows at least some people are tired of the expense and time of exurban living.

Look to Seattle for an example of needed foresight. It's nearly finished with its 1996 expansion to its commuter rail network, and just in time. Last year [2007], ridership shot up 28 percent—the highest rate in the country.

Rejecting High-Speed Rail Systems Is a Mistake Given Rising Gas Prices

Rob Kerth

Rob Kerth is a policy analyst with the Frontier Group, a public policy organization that works for a cleaner environment and a fairer and more democratic society.

Last Friday [March 4, 2011], Florida Gov. Rick Scott officially drove the nail in the coffin of the proposed high-speed rail line from Tampa to Orlando. The decision to reject $2.4 billion in federal funds for the line was, according to Scott, all about the money—specifically, the desire to protect Floridians from what he believed would be inevitable cost overruns and operating subsidies for the train.

Just how big those overruns would be, or whether they would exist at all, is a point of some contention. Scott relied on the ideologically driven Reason Institute's estimate of a potential $3 billion cost overrun in rejecting the high-speed rail line. His claim that the train would require ongoing taxpayer support once it began running, meanwhile, conflicts with an independent study released Wednesday by the Florida Department of Transportation which concluded that, far from needing a subsidy, the Tampa-to-Orlando line would have produced operating surpluses as large as $29 million per year within a decade.

But for the sake of argument, let's assume that Scott is right and Floridians do end up on the hook for $3 billion in the process of building a state-of-the-art high-speed rail system. What does that really mean?

One way to understand it is to consider that Floridians drive more than 190 billion miles every year—an average of roughly 10,500 miles per person. That amount of driving requires roughly 8.5 billion gallons of gasoline. That means that every time gas prices rise 35 cents, Floridians pay out an extra $3 billion annually for gas—the same as the high-end estimate Governor Scott gave for cost overruns from the rail project.

By failing to invest in transportation alternatives like high-speed rail, we are consigning Americans to further dependence on fossil fuels.

As it turns out, last week gas prices rose by 19 cents—the second largest 1-week increase since 1990. And since Valentine's Day, gas prices have increased by more than 40 cents. In other words, if gas prices remain at their current levels, Floridians will face a $3 billion hit to their pocketbooks this year—only instead of that money going toward the construction of clean, cutting-edge transportation that creates jobs and boosts the Florida economy, it will instead find its way into the pockets of multinational oil companies and the coffers of countries from Saudi Arabia to Venezuela.

Shortsighted Decisions

Rick Scott isn't the only governor making shortsighted decisions about high-speed rail. When Wisconsin's Governor Scott Walker rejected funding for high-speed rail in his state, he cited the expected $8 million annual operating subsidy as the reason for his cancellation. Wisconsinites drove 58 billion miles in 2009, consuming about 2.5 billion gallons of gas in the process. That means that over the course of a year, Wisconsinites pay out an extra $8 million dollars if the price of gas rises 0.3 cents.

At times of fiscal distress, its fully appropriate for public officials to be careful about the expenditure of public funds.

But it is important to remember that inaction is a form of action, and that by failing to invest in transportation alternatives like high-speed rail, we are consigning Americans to further dependence on fossil fuels—and further exposure to oil price spikes like the ones this winter.

High-speed rail makes sense. By refusing to invest in it when they have the chance, Governors Scott and Walker are keeping their states at the mercy of gas prices. If the governors really want to look out for the financial best interests of their constituents, it's time to stop making penny-wise, pound-foolish choices, and make the critical investments that will pay off for their states over the long term.

Increases in Public Transportation Use Are Shortlived

Owen McShane

Owen McShane is director of the Centre for Resource Management Studies, an organization established to educate the public about planning issues and promote quality planning projects in New Zealand.

Since the oil spike in the early seventies, enthusiasts for public transport have predicted that high prices for petrol would trigger a public transport revolution as people finally broke their "addiction" to the motor car and changed their travel mode to buses and trains.

Since then, price bubbles have increased public transport use, and lowered car miles traveled. But these changes have proved to be short-lived. More drive more.

Yet standard theory says that people respond to prices. Surely people should respond to increased petrol prices by changing their mode of travel. But why hasn't it happened in the past? More importantly, will it magically happen in the future?

Many Responses to Higher Gas Prices

The answer is that most drivers do respond to increased oil prices but they have many choices as to how to respond. You may switch to public transport provided it takes you where you want to go at a reasonable price. The problem is that part of the "reasonable price" includes the price of the increased time it takes to get to the final destination. Also, surveys reveal

Owen McShane, "The Public Transport Revolution—Why Does It Never Arrive?," *New Geography*, May 1, 2011. www.newgeography.com. Copyright © 2011 by *New Geography*. All rights reserved. Reproduced by permission.

that when people climb into their car at the end of the day they feel they have actually arrived at "home." Bus and train travel significantly defers their arrival in their own private space.

So, given time, people change their behaviour in many ways, so as to maintain the comfort, convenience, and overall efficiency of the car. For example:

1. They may decide to buy a smaller or more fuel-efficient car.

2. They may relocate either their home or their job to reduce travel costs and times—provided the land market is flexible.

3. If the local land-market is inflexible they may move to another town, or another country.

4. They may modify all their travel behaviour by better trip planning, commuter car-pooling (with prioritized parking) and general ride and task sharing.

5. They may choose to telecommute, car-pool, park-share, and ride-share.

People know how they want to live and they value their personal mobility.

Fuel costs are only a small component of total motoring costs. Cars today are lasting longer, are more reliable, are cheaper to run, and are kept in use longer. When oil was cheaper total costs of motoring were higher. That's one reason why we are driving more.

Sudden spikes in petrol prices do affect the transportation modal split, but these spikes carry less significance than media reports would suggest, and tend to be of much shorter duration than the advocates of transportation revolution predict. People know how they want to live and they value their personal mobility.

No Time for Massive Investments in Public Transit

This is not a trivial issue because [local government] councils ... are demanding that government funds massive investments in public transport because of the current oil spike, the upward blip in public transport use, and of course "Peak Oil."

The Peak Oil pessimists seem to believe no alternative to the petrol driven car exists. They also seem to ignore the increasing evidence of vast oil and gas reserves being discovered from everywhere, the eastern Mediterranean to the shores off Brazil and the American Great Plains.

A host of emerging technologies will more than compensate for any increase in the price of oil-based fuels—even for vehicles that continue to run on fossil fuels. Think of the hybrid car topping up the batteries from solar panels in the roof. Robot cars and electronically convoyed trucks hugely increase lane capacity. There are so many it would need another column to list them. The pessimists complain that it will take far too long to ring such changes in the vehicle fleet. In the next breath they talk about reshaping the urban-form, mainly by the densification of our major cities. Short of another Luftwaffe arriving on the scene, such urban renewal is hardly likely to happen overnight. Technology churns faster than cities. Try buying a Gestetner, a Telex machine, a slide rule, or a film for your camera.

Urban economist, Anthony Downs, writing in "Still Stuck in Traffic?" reminds us:

> "... trying to decrease traffic congestion by raising residential densities is like trying to improve the position of a painting hung too high on the living room wall by jacking up the ceiling instead of moving the painting."

Yet [governments] throughout the affluent world, seem determined to raise the ceilings—with no regard for costs.

The Need for More Roads

One of the arguments used against building more roads—and especially against more motorways—is that as soon as they are built they become congested again because of "induced demand." Such "induced demand" is surely the natural expression of suppressed demand. It seems unlikely that motorists will mindlessly drive between different destinations for no other reason than they can.

This is the time to invest in an enhanced roading network while making incremental investments in flexible public transport.

However, let us accept for a moment that "induced demand" is real, and suggests that improving the road network is a fruitless exercise. Advocates of expensive rail networks claim they will reduce congestion on the roads and improve the lot of private vehicle users as a consequence.

But surely, if the construction of an expensive rail network does reduce congestion on the roads then induced demand will rapidly restore the status quo. Maybe the theory is sound after all. It would explain why no retrofitted rail networks have anywhere resulted in reduced congestion.

This is the time to invest in an enhanced roading network while making incremental investments in flexible public transport. Roads can be shared by buses, trucks, vans, cars, taxis, shuttle-buses, motor-cycles and cyclists—unless compulsive regulators say they are for buses only. Railway lines can be used only by trains and if we build them in the wrong place they soon run empty. The Romans built roads and we still use them.

In a techno-novel published in 1992, [author] Michael Crichton pauses in his narrative to explain what an email is. That's not long ago.

The one certainty is that the internet/computer world will have the same impact on transport as it has already had on communications. Transport deals with bits while communication deals with bytes.

The end result will be a similar blurring of the line between public and private transport that has already happened between public and private communication. The outcomes are beyond our imagination.

We should get used to it, and realise that making cities more expensive and harder to get around in does not make them more liveable.

Recession Hits Transit Budgets Despite Rising Need

Bob Salsberg

Bob Salsberg is a reporter for The Associated Press, *a US-based global news agency.*

Boston—On a chilly evening last February, a commuter train bound for Worcester, Mass., broke down outside Boston, transforming passengers' usual 80-minute commute into a four-hour nightmare.

The train's failure was among the winter lowlights for the Boston-area commuter rail system's fleet of 80 aging locomotives which, among other woes, have had trouble starting, keeping auxiliary power functioning for lighting systems and maintaining enough air pressure for braking systems, according to transit officials.

"I can't rely on it at all," said Frank Summers, who has been commuting to Boston from suburban Ashland for about seven years and believes service is declining. "It's always jammed-packed and rarely on time."

The commuter trains are run by a firm under a contract with the Massachusetts Bay Transportation Authority, known in Boston as the T. The T's equipment woes are hardly uncommon for big-city systems, and its financial struggles are shared by almost every transit system in the U.S., big and small.

The Great Recession and cuts in government subsidies have wreaked havoc on mass transit in America, even as rising gasoline prices have pushed up demand for reliable service. By one survey, more than 80 percent of U.S. transit systems had cut service, raised fares or both since the economic downturn started.

Cash-strapped and debt-ridden systems have put off new equipment purchases and other upgrades as they struggle to maintain daily operations. The Federal Transit Administration has pointed to tens of billions of dollars in deferred maintenance, a problem particularly acute for older urban systems.

William Millar, president of the Association of Public Transportation Agencies, said there are signs of financial improvement, but it's not enough to make up for the needs.

"We still have a significant majority of systems that are still running unfunded deficits, that are still going to have to consider further fare increases and further service cuts, though they certainly don't want to do those things," he said.

More riders represent a mixed bag for operators. Fare revenue goes up, of course, but the gains can easily be offset by the higher fuel costs that systems must incur.

Especially when ridership is growing. In Boston, for example, ridership is up 5 percent from last year. In an attempt to keep pace, the T bought two new commuter rail locomotives this year—the first new ones in 20 years—and is pledging to continue efforts to modernize the line, which includes the nation's oldest subway system.

"Almost universally, across the political spectrum, people are saying rising gas prices are making them nervous, that they really want to have more and better transit options," said David Goldberg, communications director for Transportation of America, a coalition representing the interests of transit users.

More riders represent a mixed bag for operators. Fare revenue goes up, of course, but the gains can easily be offset by the higher fuel costs that systems must incur.

An influx of riders also might generate greater political support for mass transit, but the added strain on aging and overtaxed equipment could frustrate commuters and leave them ready to return to their cars when gas prices ease.

A 2009 Federal Transit Administration study that examined the "state of good repair" of the nation's seven largest rail transit agencies—New York, Boston, Philadelphia, Washington, Chicago, San Francisco and the New Jersey Transit System—found anything but good repair.

The report found that 35 percent of all rail assets of those agencies were in subpar condition. Another 35 percent were deemed adequate, and only 30 percent were in good or excellent condition. Upgrades would cost the seven largest systems $50 billion, the agency estimated.

Add in the rest of the country's public transit systems, and the maintenance backlog mushrooms to $78 billion.

Millar's group surveyed its 1,500 agencies and found that at least 40 percent were delaying capital improvements.

"The problem is to try to keep fares to a reasonable level, to try to keep services at a reasonable level, they have had to let some maintenance practices slip," he said. "Of course they are concerned about safety, so they try hard not to defer anything of a major safety need."

It's not just the major systems that are being forced to scrimp.

The Transit Authority of River City, which provides bus service for five counties in the greater Louisville, Ky., region, laid off 42 operators and mechanics last year and 10 administrative employees the previous year.

The authority's executive director, J. Barry Barker, said the system also was forced to reduce service and raise fares by $1 to $2.50 for express buses. Preventing further cuts or steeper fare hikes has meant sacrificing some improvements.

"The feds have a guideline that you can replace a full-size, 40-foot bus every 12 years. Basically I don't know anybody in the business who is replacing them after 12 years, and it's typically 14–16 (years)," he said.

Over the last several years, the authority has purchased only about half the replacement buses needed to meet even the longer cycle.

Federal support for mass transit comes largely in the form of the gasoline tax, with 2.86 cents per gallon of the federal tax earmarked for transit. But revenue has been declining as fewer Americans drive and many who do have switched to more fuel-efficient vehicles.

Federal funding also has strings attached.

The financial crunch has prompted creative approaches to generate additional money for transit systems.

Transit systems in larger cities can apply it only toward capital improvements, while systems in areas with populations of 200,000 or less can use federal money to pay operating expenses. Federal stimulus money, now ending, provided a short-term boost with 1,072 grants worth $8.8 billion for special transit projects. That included the purchase of new buses and rail cars, according to the Federal Transit Administration.

Going to the ballot box has become a popular tool for systems trying to raise revenue, and voters have generally seemed receptive.

In 2010, voters nationwide approved 73 percent of transportation-related ballot questions, many calling for increases in sales or property taxes.

In Missouri, St. Joseph boasts of having one the nation's oldest public transit systems, dating to when horses pulled large coaches before the Civil War. But with revenue falling and costs increasing for fuel, health insurance and liability coverage, the system had to go to local voters for a one-quarter cent sales tax increase in 2008 to avoid shutting down some of its eight bus routes.

But it may be only a temporary patch.

"We raised our sales tax, but the people haven't been buying as much stuff. It's not producing the revenue we would have hoped," said Andrew Clements, assistant director for St. Joseph public works. "As the future looms, eight to 10 years from now, we may be looking at a much harder challenge."

The public transit system serving Grand Rapids, Mich., won voter approval of property tax measures in 2000, 2003 and 2007—allowing it to expand from 63 buses in 1999 to 105 buses this year at peak hours and more than double its ridership, said Peter Varga, chief executive officer of The Rapid.

The agency hasn't run a deficit in a decade, nor has it increased fares or cut service, he said, even as Michigan's economy has tanked.

The financial crunch has prompted creative approaches to generate additional money for transit systems.

To help close a projected $127 million operating deficit, the Boston-area system adopted a plan to sell bonds secured by future parking revenue and use proceeds to help cover operating expenses and pay off future debt. The agency also plans to sell more advertising space at stations and on trains and buses, and is moving its unionized employees to a more flexible state-run health insurance plan.

Passengers no longer will get a free ride if their bus or train is more than a half-hour late, but fare hikes, for now at least, are off the table.

Historically, fares have accounted for 30 percent to 40 percent of total transit revenue nationwide.

Experts who point to more modern and reliable systems around the world say U.S. cities must find ways to overcome financial hurdles and invest in public transit.

In Los Angeles, voters agreed in 2008 to pay a half-cent sales tax over the next 30 years to fund a massive expansion of public transportation. But Mayor Antonio Villaraigosa doesn't want to wait that long for the projects to be completed, so he's proposed borrowing billions from the federal government so the work can be done in just a decade.

"It's becoming clear that (cities) have to remain healthy and vital, and it's also becoming increasingly clear that a functioning transit system is a big part of that," said Robert Puentes, a transportation expert with the Brookings Institution.

Cuts in Federal Public Transportation Funding Could Further Limit Mass Transit

Keith Laing

Keith Laing is a reporter for The Hill, *a congressional newspaper that publishes daily whenever the US Congress is in session.*

Transportation advocates are wasting no time trying to convince lawmakers not to cut spending on public transit systems.

Though they have already secured stable funding through March of next year [2012], public transportation groups are worried Congress could impose significant cuts in a long-term highway bill, which would include public transportation funding.

On Tuesday [September 20, 2011], rallies were staged across subway and bus systems around the country to alert passengers to the potential cuts, dubbed "Don't X out public transit."

"Safe, reliable public transit is at risk," American Public Transportation Association President William Millar said Tuesday on a conference call with reporters.

Proposed Cuts in Public Transit

House Republicans have proposed a long-term bill that would maintain the same 80 percent-to-20 percent split between highway projects and public transportation funding, but would reduce overall spending to about $35 billion per year.

Transit advocates argue that would cut their portion of the budget pie by as much as a third, resulting in the loss of 620,000 transportation jobs in both the public and private sectors.

They also say such cuts would imperil daily commutes in cities large and small across the country at a time when passengers are already paying more for rides and communities are being forced to cut back services.

"We've already seen the highest fare increases and worst service cuts in 60 years," John Robert Smith, president and CEO of Reconnecting America and co-chairman of Transportation for America, said Tuesday.

The American Public Transportation Association and the Amalgamated Transit Union were also involved in Tuesday's effort.

The groups might not have to worry about further cuts for the time being.

The stagnant economy had already taken a broad hit on public transit funding at the local level. Budget cuts from Congress would only make matters worse.

Congress last week approved legislation to extend highway and aviation funding through March of next year. That bill would expire just as lawmakers are focusing more and more on the 2012 campaign, leading some to think further short-term extensions are likely.

But that isn't stopping public transportation groups from making their case now.

Smith said that the stagnant economy had already taken a broad hit on public transit funding at the local level. Budget cuts from Congress would only make matters worse, he said.

"Some may think we can't afford to invest in transit," Smith said. "I think the question is, can we afford not to?"

Long-Term Funding Issues

The House proposal for a long-term bill would spend $235 billion over six years on highways and public transit. GOP [Republican] lawmakers argue this figure is equal to the dollars raised by the federal gas tax, which is authorized by the highway bill.

The Senate has suggested a shorter, two-year, $109 billion bill, which increases current levels of funding for inflation.

Given the political climate, some think a long-term deal is not within reach, but Millar said political considerations could help advocates make their case.

"It's fashionable in Washington to look at the political season as negative, but most congressmen and senators are going to want to go home and say, 'I did something,'" he said in an interview with *The Hill*. "I don't know many congressmen who are going to want to go home and say, 'Guess what? I just cut the road budget by 30 percent.'"

While lawmakers face serious hurdles in winning a longer-term transportation bill, the issues aren't quite as thorny as the labor dispute that bogged down an extension of the Federal Aviation Administration's [FAA] authorization.

Mostly because of labor disputes, lawmakers have approved 22 short-term extensions of the FAA bill.

Asked if the highway bill might follow that pattern, Millar could only say he hoped not.

"I certainly hope we don't get to 22 extensions," he said. "To paraphrase an old TV show, I think eight is enough."

Millar said he was optimistic because "the issues are well-known" involving the transportation bill, and Democratic leaders in the Senate and Republican leaders in the House were personally involved in the short-term extension.

"I saw it as a good sign that Majority Leader [Harry] Reid [D-Nev.] and Speaker [John] Boehner [R-Ohio] were able to get together and get a six-month extension," he said. "I think that's a very good sign."

High-Speed Rail
Is Too Expensive

Joel Kotkin

Joel Kotkin is a writer and author, a distinguished presidential fellow in urban futures at Chapman University in Orange, California, and executive editor of www.newgeography.com, a website that focuses on economic development, metropolitan demographics, and community leadership.

Perhaps nothing so illustrates President [Barack] Obama's occasional disconnect with reality than his fervent advocacy of high-speed rail. Amid mounting pressure for budget cuts that affect existing programs, including those for the inner city, the president has made his $53 billion proposal to create a national high-speed rail network as among his top priorities.

Our President may be an intelligent and usually level-headed man, but this represents a serious case of policy delusion. As Robert Samuelson pointed out in *Newsweek*, high-speed rail is not an appropriate fit for a country like the U.S. Except for a few areas, notably along the Northeast Corridor, the U.S. just lacks the density that would make such a system work. Samuelson calls the whole idea "a triumph of fancy over fact."

Extraordinary Costs

Arguably the biggest problem with high-speed rail is its extraordinary costs, which would require massive subsidies to keep operating. Unlike the Federal Highway Program, largely financed by the gas tax, high-speed rail lacks any credible source of funding besides taxpayer dollars.

Joel Kotkin, "Obama's High-Speed Rail Obsession," *Forbes*, February 18, 2011. www.forbes.com. Copyright © 2011 by Forbes Media LLC. All rights reserved. Reprinted by permission of Forbes Media LLC.

Part of the pitch for high-speed rail is nationalistic. To be a 21st century super power, we must emulate current No. 2 China. But this is a poor reason to indulge in a hugely expensive program when the U.S. already has the world's most evolved highway, freight rail and airline system.

The prospect of mounting and uncontrollable costs has led governors to abandon high-speed projects in Ohio, Wisconsin and most recently Florida, where a battle to save the Tampa-Orlando line has begun.

Also, if the U.S. were to follow the Chinese model, as some have suggested, perhaps it should impose rule from a Washington version of a centralized authoritarian government. After all, dictatorships are often quite adept at "getting things done." But in a democracy "getting things done" means balancing interests and efficiencies, not following orders from above.

In China high-speed rail is so costly that the trains are too expensive for the average citizen. Furthermore, construction costs are so high the Chinese Academy of Sciences has already warned that its debts may not be payable. This experience with ballooning costs and far lower fare revenues have raised taxpayer obligations in Taiwan and Korea and added to heavily to the national debt in Japan.

The prospect of mounting and uncontrollable costs has led governors to abandon high-speed projects in Ohio, Wisconsin and most recently Florida, where a battle to save the Tampa-Orlando line has begun. In times of budget stress, the idea of building something new, and historically difficult to contain by costs, becomes a hard sell.

Oddly, the leaders of California, faced with one of the worst fiscal positions in the country, are determined to spend several billions on what *Sacramento Bee* columnist Dan Walters has dubbed a train to nowhere for 54 miles between Madera and Corcoran—two unremarkable and remote Central Valley towns. The proposal makes the former Alaska Sen. Ted Stevens' notorious "bridges to nowhere" project seem like frugal public policy.

California's train to nowhere has been justified as part of [a] wider project to construct a statewide system. But the whole idea makes little financial sense: The University of California's Institute for Transportation describes the high-speed proposal as based on an "inconsistent model" whose ridership projections are simply not "reliable."

Equally suspect are cost estimates, which have doubled (after adjustment for inflation) from 1999 to $42.6 billion last year and a new study says that the project could currently cost close to $65 billion. Costs for a ticket from Los Angeles to San Francisco, originally pegged at $55 one way, had nearly doubled by 2009, and now some estimates place it at about ... $100 or perhaps [as] much as $190—considerably more than an advanced-purchase ticket on far faster Southwest Airlines.

There's growing political opposition to the system as well, and not just among penny-pinching right-wingers. Residents and local officials in the San Francisco peninsula, a wealthy and reliably liberal portion of Silicon Valley, largely oppose plans to route the line through their communities. This includes some prominent liberal legislators, such as San Mateo's Assembly member Jerry Hill, who has threatened to put high-speed rail back on the ballot if costs start to surpass initial estimates. Another Democrat, California Treasurer Bill Lockyer has doubts that the rail authority will be able to sell the deal to potential bond-buyers—due in part to a lack of consistent estimates in ridership or cost.

Powerful Supporters of High-Speed Rail

So why is Obama still so determined to push the high-speed boondoggle? Largely it's a deadly combination of theology and money. Powerful rail construction interests, notably the German giant Siemens, are spreading cash like mustard on a bratwurst to promote the scheme. Add to that construction unions and the ever voracious investment banks who would love to pocket fees for arranging to sell the bonds and you have interests capable of influencing either party.

High-speed rail is far more expensive than such things as fixing current commuter rail and subways or expanding both public and private bus service.

Then there's what might be called the "density lobby"— big city mayors, construction firms and the urban land owners. These magnates, who frequently extort huge public subsidies for their projects, no doubt think it grand to spend billions of public funds on something that might also increase the value of their real estate.

And finally there are the true believers, notably planners, academics, green activists and an army of rail fans. These are people who believe America should be more like Europe— denser, more concentrated in big cities and tied to the rails. "High speed rail is not really about efficient transport," notes California transit expert and accountant Tom Rubin. "It's all about shaping cities for a certain agenda."

A Chorus of Opposition

Yet despite their power, these forces face mounting obstacles. As transportation expert Ken Orski points out, the balance of power in the House [of Representatives] now lies with suburban and rural legislators, whose constituents would not benefit much from high-speed rail. And then there are governors, increasingly Republican and conservative, very anxious not to add potentially huge obligations to their already stressed budgets.

The most decisive opposition, however, could come from those who favor transit spending but understand the need to prioritize. High-speed rail is far more expensive than such things as fixing current commuter rail and subways or expanding both public and private bus service. Indeed, the money that goes to urban rail often ends up being diverted from other, more cost-effective systems, notably buses.

The choice between high-speed rail and more conventional, less expensive transit has already been presaged in the fight against expanding LA's expensive rail system by organizations representing bus riders. These activists contend that rail swallows funds that could be spent on buses

Much the same case is being made [in] the San Francisco peninsula. The opponents of high-speed rail on the San Francisco peninsula are outraged that the state would spend billions on a chancy potential boondoggle when the popular Caltrain commuter rail service is slated to be curtailed or even eliminated.

One can of course expect that anti-spending conservatives will be the biggest cheerleaders for high-speed rail's decline. But transit advocates may be forced to join the chorus of opposition, in order to steer transit spending towards more basic priorities [such] as buses in Los Angeles, subways in New York or commuter rail in the San Francisco Bay Area.

In an era of tough budgets, and proposed cutbacks on basic services, setting sensible transportation priorities is crucial. Spending billions on a conveyance that will benefit a relative handful of people and places is not just illogical. It's obscene.

CHAPTER 4

What Are the Keys to Oil and Gasoline Independence?

Chapter Preface

American President Barack Obama has identified energy independence as a major goal of his administration's energy policy. However, the president is also concerned about the environment and carbon emissions that contribute to global warming, so he has sought to achieve energy independence mainly by boosting alternative and clean energy technologies rather than by focusing solely on increasing the nation's production of fossil fuels such as oil and natural gas. Supporters see the Obama administration's energy positions as visionary because the United States can never drill enough oil to be free from foreign imports. Critics, on the other hand, think the Obama energy plan is a disaster and argue that alternative fuels are decades away and that America must seek to produce as much oil and natural gas as possible for the near future to minimize the nation's reliance on foreign producers. The issue may be somewhat moot, because the country's economic problems and debt crisis have made most of the administration's energy ideas impossible to achieve, at least during the president's first term.

President Obama was successful, however, in funding some clean energy projects during his first year in office. For example, Obama included a number of energy initiatives in the American Recovery and Reinvestment Act of 2009 (ARRA)—legislation enacted in response to the economic crisis then facing the country. The Act's purpose was to create jobs, spur economic activity, and fund long-term US investments in infrastructure. Many of the projects included in the law were for the development of clean energy and clean transportation—that is, renewable, low-carbon or emissions-free energy, such as solar, wind, and biofuels. According to some reports, the Act contained $70 billion in direct spending and tax credits for these types of projects.

One of the biggest ARRA-funded projects, for example, was a $3.4 billion Smart Grid Investment Grant designed to help utility companies and others to improve the US electrical grid. The program provided federal assistance to cover up to 50 percent of investments in so-called smart grid technologies with the goal of making the electrical system more efficient and more flexible in responding to energy demands. For example, a digitized grid would connect rural energy producers with urban power grids and would allow power companies to better manage demands for energy, by cutting electricity to non-essential uses during certain times of the day or during demand surges. Smart grid technology also would be better able to deliver electricity from various renewable sources and to accommodate new green technologies, such as plug-in electric cars. Smart grid technology, supporters also hope, will help repel security threats, such as cyber attacks, on the US electrical grid.

Another priority in ARRA was the Advanced Research Projects Agency-Energy (ARPA-E) project, which created a new government agency to promote and fund research and development of renewable energy technologies, such as solar, wind, geothermal, biofuels, and biomass energy crops. A host of related energy technologies also received grants, including energy efficiency projects, smart building technologies, and energy storage ideas, including improved lithium-ion batteries designed to power electric cars. About $400 million was budgeted for the first year, with plans to increase this to the $1 billion range in later years.

Other parts of ARRA funded a variety of additional energy initiatives. A weatherization program funded by ARRA, for example, allocated about $9.5 billion to weatherize 75 percent of federal buildings as well as more than one million private low-income homes around the country. ARRA also devoted funds to projects that train people for green jobs.

Apart from ARRA, the Obama administration also has taken several other actions to further its energy goals. The US Environmental Protection Agency (EPA) set new fuel economy standards for cars and light trucks that will raise the average fuel economy to 35.5 miles per gallon by 2016, and to 54.5 miles per gallon by 2025. The agency is also developing the first national fuel economy standards for heavier trucks, vans, and buses, designed to make those vehicles more fuel-efficient by 2018. In addition, as of January 2011, the EPA began regulating carbon emissions of companies operating in the United States as part of the Clean Air Act. The EPA was given this new authority as a result of a 2007 Supreme Court ruling granting the agency the authority to regulate emissions as a form of air pollution. Moreover, the Obama administration has suggested that it favors national Clean Energy Standards (CES) that would require 80 percent of US electrical power to be derived from zero- or low-carbon sources by 2035.

Although President Obama has also declared that environmentally friendly domestic oil production and nuclear power need to be part of the US energy mix, events have overtaken these initiatives. For example, the BP oil spill catastrophe in the Gulf of Mexico in 2010 caused President Obama to impose a moratorium on new oil drilling permits. The moratorium has been lifted but the administration still has been reluctant to issue deepwater drilling permits. Also, the president's support for nuclear power was made more difficult after the 2011 Japanese earthquake and tsunami, which destroyed the Fukushima nuclear facilities in that country. After the Japan disaster, the president continued to voice support for building more nuclear plants but this position increasingly is not supported by US public opinion because of concerns about the safety of nuclear power.

Many commentators predict that little action will be taken on energy issues given the gridlock in Congress, the focus on jobs and the national debt, and the upcoming 2012 presidential election. The president's cap-and-trade legislation died in the Senate in 2009, and his opponents in Congress have only grown more powerful since then. Unless President Obama is re-elected with majorities in both houses of Congress in 2012, many political pundits think it is unlikely that he will be able to achieve any energy goals that require legislation. Meanwhile, some opponents want to block the administration's regulatory energy efforts, such as the EPA's regulation of carbon emissions as part of the Clean Air Act. The authors of the following viewpoints present some of the differing views about the ways to achieve oil and gas independence.

The United States Must Increase Domestic Oil Production

Steve Huntley

Steve Huntley is a columnist for the Chicago Sun-Times, *an American newspaper.*

Predictions of $5 a gallon gasoline this summer [2011] are a stark reminder the nation doesn't have a comprehensive or even coherent energy policy to protect our economy in these uncertain times for a reliable, low-cost oil supply.

Obsessed with climate change, President [Barack] Obama and Democrats have made green energy the golden goal of U.S. energy strategy though many technological obstacles make wind, solar, hydrogen and electrical cars as mainstays of everyday life many years or even decades away.

Oil remains the lifeblood of the economy. It fuels our cars, the transportation system for moving products, the growing of food and the manufacture of products ranging from anesthetics to ballpoint pens to clothing to lipstick to paint to refrigerators to phones and on and on. We can't do without it.

Threats to Oil Markets

Libya is a relatively minor actor in oil production and the loss of much of its output from the civil war there has been offset by a drop in demand in Japan caused by its earthquake-tsunami disaster. But the enterprising Japanese will soon be rebuilding. China's booming economy slurps up 10 percent more oil than a year ago. The slowly gathering economic recovery here and in Europe will push up oil prices.

They have risen 20 percent since the Mideast uprisings started. No one knows how long Libyan oil will be off line. More critically, the contest between Iran and Saudi Arabia in Bahrain could become destabilizing. The Bahrain affair is not a carbon copy of pro-democracy movements elsewhere but one inflamed by sectarian passions—a ruling Sunni minority against a restive, resentful Shiite majority.

Mideast unpredictability and the potential of supply interruptions demand greater domestic oil and gas output.

That imbalance also is at play in Saudi Arabia. Riyadh is helping neighboring Bahrain suppress the protest movement out of fear revolt might spread to its own Shiite population. Strife in Saudi Arabia, with its huge petroleum reserves, could wreak chaos in oil markets.

The Need to Develop Domestic Oil

Obama recently boasted that U.S. oil production is up on his watch. That's disingenuous as it takes years to bring a well in production, so we're seeing the fruits of projects begun before he took office.

This week we witnessed the incoherent picture of an American president whose administration has impeded oil production in the Gulf of Mexico promoting Brazil's program to exploit its off-shore petroleum resources. "We want to help with technology and support to develop these oil reserves safely, and when you're ready to start selling, we want to be one of your best customers," Obama told an audience in Brasilia.

Mideast unpredictability and the potential of supply interruptions demand greater domestic oil and gas output. That means not just drilling in the Gulf but also developing oil shale resources such as the Green River Formation in the West. The U.S. Geological Survey estimates it holds 1.5 trillion barrels of oil, the largest shale deposits in the world.

Rather than outsource oil jobs to Brazil, the administration should be promoting them here. It's not just good energy policy, it's sound economic strategy. These are good-paying jobs at a time when our economy needs them. For example, mean salaries for oil and gas derrick and drill workers range from $43,000 to $59,000, the Bureau of Labor Statistics reports. Measuring the full range of oil and gas exploration and production jobs shows an average salary of $96,844, more than double the average annual salary of all occupations, according to the American Petroleum Institute.

I continue to believe we need to develop transportation alternatives to oil, such as the alcohol program promoted by the Set America Free coalition. That's not the current ethanol strategy that turns corn into ethanol, raising food prices. Rather it's the production of methanol from coal, natural gas and biomass that can be used in flex-fuel cars. It costs only $100 to make new autos flex-fuel capable.

Still, our dependence on oil is inescapable. We need to develop all domestic sources until the day green energy resources become a reliable, cost-effective alternative.

Oil Independence Is Impossible So Energy Independence Must Be the Goal

Swellsman

Swellsman is a frequent, anonymous blogger on the progressive website Daily Kos.

Something we've been hearing for decades now is that America needs to achieve "energy independence." However, while both Conservatives and Liberals deploy this phrase routinely, they usually intend it to function as shorthand for two very different policy prescriptions. For Conservatives, "energy independence" generally means independence from foreign sources of oil. For Liberals, "energy independence" usually means the creation of sustainable and renewable energy sources.

The two concepts are not the same, and it is a shame that a single phrase has been used to signal both. Although it is probably too late now, our national dialogue would be much improved by using different phrases to distinguish these two positions. What Conservatives are really seeking is "Oil Independence"—the ability to have as much oil as is wanted without being subject to the whims of other nations. What Liberals are really seeking is true "Energy Independence"—the ability to have as much energy as is needed without relying on finite energy sources.

A few recent news stories clearly demonstrate that not only is Energy Independence a more idealistic concept than is simply seeking Oil Independence, it is also much more practical.

Ending Oil Dependence by Force

There are only two ways for America to sever its dependence on oil producing nations: it can either invade those countries that still have sizeable caches of oil and seize those nations' oil fields for itself, or it can boost its domestic production until that production is sufficient to meet all of America's oil needs.

Now there are many who would claim that America already has engaged in the first course of action—and there probably is something to that assertion—but this approach to Oil Independence is clearly unworkable.

First, even setting aside the basic question of morality, a war of aggression to seize oil is incredibly difficult to pull off. It cannot be done openly, because it would result in the aggressor becoming a pariah nation; say whatever you want about America's might, we still need trading partners. Which means that in order to succeed at something like that, the invading country has to find a pretext to invade a country, topple the government, and then arrange for a compliant successor government to "request" that it stay on and take over oil production (obviously, at extremely advantageous terms). This at least provides a patina of legality, but as the misadventure in Iraq proved it is incredibly difficult to occupy a country that does not really want you there.

Second, even assuming one pulls off a successful smash-n-grab on the international stage, wars of aggression are incredibly expensive ways to obtain any natural resource. What would have been cheaper? Lifting sanctions on Iraq and buying oil on the open market, or invading and occupying the country for decades while at the same time thumbing our nose at the rest of the world and declaring that Iraq's oil belongs to us now—as [business tycoon] Donald Trump actually argues we should do?

No matter how much Conservatives want to believe in "American Exceptionalism," no matter how much they may cling to the Green Lantern Theory of Geopolitics, the fact stubbornly remains (thank God) that neither America nor any other nation has the actual ability to attain Oil Independence by sheer force.

End Oil Dependence by Increasing Production

Exxon Mobile Corp. (XOM) announced it found the equivalent of 700 million barrels of oil beneath the Gulf of Mexico, the biggest discovery in the region in 12 years. The estimated size of the Hadrian field may increase as drilling continues, Exxon said in a statement today [June 16, 2011]. The discovery is about 250 miles (400 kilometers) southwest of New Orleans in 7,000 feet of water, Irving, Texas-based Exxon said. Wow! That certainly sounds big! But let's unpack those three sentences just a little.

First, let's note that the newly discovered Hadrian field is about 2,000 feet even *farther* below sea level than was the field being drilled during the Deepwater Horizon catastrophe last year. So, right there, drilling this oil field presents another possibility of ecologic catastrophe. After all, the reason it took so long to stop all of that oil gushing into the Gulf last year is because it is difficult to do pretty much *anything* that far down.

The United States needs to find about ten new domestic fields a year . . . and bring them online immediately. . . . This clearly is not going to happen.

Second, let's note the length of time that has passed since we last discovered an oil field this significant in the Gulf: 12 years. And one reason this field was not discovered earlier is almost certainly because no one had gone looking for it before; all things being equal, oil companies don't enthuse about drilling for oil a mile and a half below sea level. The only reason they are looking to drill there today is because they've essentially depleted the more easily obtainable oil located on land or in shallow water. The fact that Exxon Mobile is even looking for fields 1 ½ miles below sea level proves how finite a resource oil is. Once you've sucked your milkshake dry, the cup never magically refills; you've got to go find another one, and we've run out of cheap and easy "milkshakes" to exploit.

It doesn't necessarily mean that Exxon Mobile actually has access to 700 million barrels of oil, as it is not yet clear how much of this new find is actually recoverable. (You can never recover all of the oil out of a given field, because the pressure in an oil field decreases as the oil is pumped out of it; eventually, more than a barrel of oil's worth of energy is required to pump up a single barrel of the remaining oil.) But even if all 700 million barrels from this new find were instantly recoverable—and they are not, of course—what does that mean?

Well, according to the CIA [US Central Intelligence Agency] the United States consumed 18.69 million barrels of oil per day back in 2009. Even using this two year old figure, that means that Exxon Mobile's massive new find, the biggest in 12 years, could supply all of America's oil needs for . . . 37 days. It means that to replace all of the oil America consumes every year the United States needs to find about ten new domestic fields a year—each one the size of Exxon Mobile's new "massive" discovery—and bring them online immediately. Only then could the United States claim to have truly achieved oil independence.

This clearly is not going to happen.

Right now, global demand for oil runs to about 89 million barrels a day. Which means this is the amount of new oil that needs to be found around the world—every day—just to keep from depleting current oil reserves. Obviously, that is a tall order. For example, even if the global demand for oil were to suddenly stop rising—which it won't—Exxon Mobile's new 700 million barrel oil field would only cover about one week's worth of global consumption. For that matter, Brazil's discovery last October [2011] of a new offshore field estimated at 8 billion barrels of recoverable oil can only meet the world's needs for about 3 months.

Dealing with Peak Oil

Indeed, last year the International Energy Agency [IEA] explicitly acknowledged the fact of "peak oil"—that is, the point at which the global supply of oil maxes out and then begins an inexorable decline—and provided a best estimate as to when it expects that point to be reached: 2035. But even that date, which is only about 24 years away—may be a bit optimistic.

The good people over at Energy Bulletin reviewed the IEA's 2010 World Energy Outlook and summarized the IEA's projections for future global oil production. . . .

Extending from around 2006 until 2035, the IEA estimates that the world's supply of crude oil—that is, oil the way we normally think of it, something liquid that can be pumped out of oil fields—will remain constant. Of course, this isn't great news since global *demand* will continue to rise. But it actually gets worse.

Look at how the IEA anticipates the world will maintain this constant rate of crude oil production. To begin with, the IEA acknowledges that we have begun to see a precipitous drop in production from all currently developed oil fields. The IEA expects that some already identified but as yet undeveloped fields will make up part of this shortfall, but it also acknowledges that production from these newly developed fields will also begin to drop precipitously around 2017.

In fact, the only way the IEA is able to claim that crude oil production will just remain constant until 2035 is by asserting that both of these expected shortfalls will be made up for by *oil fields that have not yet been discovered*—like, for example,

Exxon Mobile's "massive" Hadrian oil field, which can supply the world's needs for a whole week. . . .

The IEA's projections seem an exercise in wishful thinking: "sure, all known oil fields are quickly running out of that sweet, sweet crude, but we'll find some more *somewhere*." In fact, according to its own figures the only way the International Energy Agency avoids the conclusion that "peak oil" already has occurred is by suggesting both that if we clap loudly enough new fields will be discovered *and* that "natural gas liquids" and "unconventional oil"—the really expensive kind, produced from tar sands and shales—will make up the loss.

At least, y'know, for the next 20 years or so.

The United States Must Transition to Low-Carbon Fuels

David Burwell

David Burwell is the director of the Energy and Climate Program at the Carnegie Endowment for International Peace, a private nonprofit organization dedicated to advancing cooperation among nations and promoting active international engagement by the United States.

Four-dollar-a-gallon gas inevitably elicits calls of "drill-baby-drill" to ease the pain felt in Americans' wallets. But the present debate over how to fight high gas prices and whether or not to increase domestic oil production overlooks a key point—peak U.S. oil consumption has already been reached. We are looking at things backwards. The real question is not how much the U.S. can produce locally, but how fast domestic oil demand will decline and how public policy can support this transition. Demand destruction will do more for American national security, the environment, trade balances, and jobs, than ramping up production ever could.

Signs of Reduced Demand for Oil

Green shoots prophesying accelerated declines in American oil consumption are cropping up everywhere. Even before the recession, total domestic oil consumption was in decline and the trend accelerated as the economy lagged. And, importantly, the recovery has not led to the expected increase in consumption. The Energy Information Agency reports that gasoline consumption has declined for sixteen straight weeks compared to sales a year ago. Last week, the year-over-year weekly decline was 3.7 percent. While total travel has bounced back a bit as the economy has picked up, the most important measure of what's happening, vehicle miles traveled per capita, continues to decline.

U.S. vehicle sales also portend increasing declines in oil consumption. In 2008, auto sales, in the face of $4 gas and economic troubles, crashed to nine million vehicles annually. In the first quarter of 2011 they bounced back to a new rate of 13 million vehicles annually as consumers abandoned their gas guzzlers for Detroit's new line of gas sippers. As a result, the economy is exhibiting remarkable resilience amid this new oil price spike. President [Barack] Obama's directive that the entire federal vehicle fleet will be fuel efficient or rely on alternative fuels by 2015 will accelerate this transition.

Consumers are already "producing" new oil by reducing their need for it.

Oil and gas companies are also beginning to demonstrate new doubts about overreliance on oil. Even as oil prices—and profits—rise, windfall earnings are being re-invested more widely. ExxonMobil is only replacing 90 percent of the oil it produces through exploration or acquisition of new oil reserves, instead significantly increasing its investment in natural gas, algae, and other biofuels. BP is doing the same, announcing this week [May 26, 2011] an investment in Verdezyne, maker of a yeast that converts plant sugars to biofuels. Total, the big French oil company, has just bought a 60 percent interest in Sunpower, the largest U.S. solar energy company.

Regulatory policy is also nudging the energy industry off oil. New standards for fuel efficiency and renewable fuels mean that it doesn't take a chemical engineer to understand that oil, the source of 95 percent of transportation fuel, is about to face heavy competition in the fuels market.

Perhaps the most significant incentive driving reduction in oil demand is the price of oil itself. While current prices might be a short-term trend, long-term prices will remain high due to the rapid pace of motorization in China, India, and other developing countries. High world oil prices, while painful at the pump, accelerate turnover to a low-carbon vehicle fleet which, in turn, help reduce the marginal cost of travel even at higher fuel prices.

Moving Away from Oil

With the progress that has already been made, the choice is easy. Transitioning to low-carbon fuels and improving vehicle and system efficiency, promises higher returns in oil independence in the short term than a focus on increasing domestic production that only drains America's reserves faster.

Washington can [reduce demand] ... by intensifying its efforts to increase fuel efficiency, establishing a low carbon fuel standard, investing in more travel choices, and ending subsidized sprawl.

Consider this: if America fully exploited all its known reserves to meet 100 percent of its domestic needs we would run out of oil within four years. Yes, we have more domestic oil to discover but we are increasingly tapped out on the production side.

History, as well as basic economics, demonstrates that increased domestic oil production does not necessarily lower prices for American consumers. After several years of aggressive incentives to boost domestic production, the percentage of oil the United States imports is 15 percent lower than it was in 2005 though the price of oil has doubled to over $100 a barrel. Obviously, further increases in domestic production will have little to no impact on gasoline prices.

Washington can accelerate demand destruction by intensifying its efforts to increase fuel efficiency, establishing a low carbon fuel standard, investing in more travel choices, and ending subsidized sprawl. It could also extend an olive branch to oil companies by offering to trade oil subsidies for investment tax credits in renewables, or by encouraging pooled energy R&D [research and development] efforts as it is already doing with China. The fact that oil companies are already testing the waters for alternative energy investments indicates that they may be ready to step up their efforts.

The road to oil independence is clear and straight: better to water the green shoots of demand destruction than feed our oil addiction through the chimera of "drill-baby-drill."

The United States Must Promote Electric Vehicles to Achieve Freedom from Oil

Sarah Hodgdon

Sarah Hodgdon is the director of conservation for the Sierra Club, an American environmental organization.

Imagine greater security for our service members abroad. Imagine freedom from the rising prices of the gas pump. Imagine freedom from massive oil spills like the one last year [2010] in the Gulf of Mexico or the one last week [July 1, 2011] in Yellowstone National Park. Imagine freedom from auto tailpipe emissions. Imagine greater economic freedom through reduced national debt and thousands of new clean tech jobs. Imagine freedom from oil altogether.

Promoting Electric Vehicles

This week, an unlikely group of more than 180 companies and organizations—large and small—from nearly every U.S. state joined together to issue a statement asking for comprehensive local, state, and federal programs that will promote plug-in electric vehicles (EVs) and drive us toward freedom from oil. This statement makes it clear more than ever before that there is widespread support for EVs in every part of the country and from a diverse set of economic, security, job growth, environmental, and public health interests.

Look at what our oil dependence is subjecting Americans to: The U.S. armed forces spend up to $83 billion annually protecting vulnerable infrastructure and patrolling oil transit routes. Earlier this year US Navy Secretary Roy Mabus said that "out of every 24 fuel convoys we use [in Afghanistan], a soldier or marine is killed or wounded guarding that convoy. That's a high price to pay for fuel."

Our nation sends up to a third of a trillion dollars overseas each year to purchase foreign oil, often produced by countries that are unstable or unfriendly to American interests. Foreign oil purchases are also responsible for about 50% of the U.S. trade deficit.

New EVs are on the market in select cities nationwide, and by next year, they will be available in nearly every state.

The statement we issued this week on freedom from oil includes companies and organizations with leaders who have served in our Armed Services—such as Brian Patnoe, Vice President of Fleet Sales at CODA Automotive, a Los Angeles, CA-based electric vehicle and battery company.

"I'm proud to be working for a company committed to supporting oil independence and the emerging EV supply chain," said Patnoe. "As a former Marine, it's also exciting for me to see successful business opportunities that support a prosperous oil-free future—from CODA's own parts manufacturers and assembly line workers to electrical workers installing EV chargers and the customers purchasing a whole new type of vehicle."

Necessary Policies

New EVs are on the market in select cities nationwide, and by next year, they will be available in nearly every state. Now, we need to put the right policies, infrastructure, and programs in place to support a cleaner and safer shift in the way we power our vehicles. This week's EV sign-on statement spells out some of the types of policies that will allow us to become EV-ready ASAP:

1. *Expand national, regional, and local efforts that help attract greater concentrations of electric vehicles in communities across the country.*

2. *Remove unnecessary bureaucratic and market obstacles to vehicle electrification nationwide through a variety of policies that:*

   - bolster nationwide installation of and access to basic charging infrastructure, both at people's homes and in public places;

   - incentivize the purchase of electric vehicles and EV charging equipment and streamline the permitting application process for EV charging equipment;

   - educate the public about the benefits of EVs and the costs, opportunities, and logistical considerations involved with EV charging infrastructure;

   - ensure appropriate training for workers installing EV charging equipment and for first responders;

   - encourage utilities to provide attractive rates and programs for EV owners and increase off-peak charging;

   - assist in deployment of clean energy, efficiency, and energy management technologies jointly with vehicle charging; and

   - accelerate advanced battery cost reduction by boosting EV use in fleets, in second use, and in stationary applications.

3. *Ensure US leadership in manufacturing of electric drive vehicles, batteries and components.*

EVs will help us achieve freedom from oil, and they also mean less air pollution. Emissions from EVs are at least 30% lower than those from traditional vehicles—and that's on today's electric grid. As we clean up our grid and rely more and more on renewable sources of power, EVs get even cleaner over time.

Natural Gas-Powered Vehicles Should Be the First Step Toward Energy Independence

David Fessler

David Fessler is the energy and infrastructure expert for Investment U, a website that publishes a daily newsletter and provides other products to help investors.

Why isn't the U.S. government doing more to get us off foreign oil?

Great question. It's one I ask myself all the time.

It was clearly on the minds of many attendees at the Investment U Conference in San Diego a couple of weeks ago [March 2010], too. I lost count of the number of times people asked me about it—and what the United States should be doing to address the problem.

So I decided to see what it would take to drastically cut our oil dependence.

How could we get to the point where we could get by on the oil we have here? To get to the point where it wouldn't be necessary to import it from anyone. Not even Canada. . . .

Getting America Off Foreign Oil . . . Now

Let's start with a few "crude" facts:

- The world produces about 85 million barrels of oil per day (BPD).

- Of that amount, the United States uses 25%, or about 21 million BPD.

- Breaking that down even further, the transportation sector gobbles up about 70% of the United States' daily use, or 14.7 million BPD.

Now, here's the crux of it. . . .

- We import about 75% of what we use, or about 16 million BPD. So it's easy to see that if the transportation sector can switch from oil to other fuels, we can get rid of 93% of our oil imports. But how?

The Mandate That Could Solve America's Oil Dependence Problem

When you think about the U.S. Congress, "energy" isn't the first thing that springs to mind.

And when it comes to the energy sector, our elected officials in Washington are in a collective slumber.

But let's assume for a crazy second that in a stroke of simplicity and common sense, Congress issues a mandate to all vehicle manufacturers.

The Mandate:

- Of the 10 million cars, SUVs, light trucks and heavy-duty trucks that will be produced in 2012, a minimum of 5% will operate on natural gas. (This is a much easier design issue than an all-electric vehicle, by the way.)

- It will also give auto manufacturers a tax credit of $1,000 per car over the first five years.

- Manufacturers must also increase their natural gas-powered vehicle production by 5% per year, with the goal that by 2015, natural gas will power 20% of all vehicles produced.

- The mandate increases by 20% per year, so that by 2019, all new vehicles produced will run on natural gas.

In Ten Years, America's Oil Imports Could Be Dramatically Reduced

The total U.S. vehicle fleet is roughly 254 million. Of that, 135 million are cars, 99 million are SUVs and/or pickup trucks and roughly nine million are larger trucks.

And with that mandate in place, 10 years from now, vehicles that run on natural gas will have replaced 76% of all the gasoline and diesel vehicles.

The result?

- We'll have shaved at least 13.8 million BPD—about 86%—off our daily oil imports.

- Our annual trade deficit will drop by about $94 billion, or 25%.

And what about the $10 billion in incentives that the government would shell out to auto companies?

We could phase in a progressive "legacy fuel" tax on gasoline and diesel to offset the tax incentives. It could either be phased out after five years, or left in place to continue to discourage gasoline and diesel use. That would hasten the switch to natural gas.

Of course, with all these natural gas vehicles, we'll need places to refuel them. So the 167,000 gas stations across the United States will need natural gas pumps alongside the gasoline ones.

In that regard, the government would offer incentives to gas station operators, right along with the ones to auto companies.

That means companies like Clean Energy Fuels can step up right now and begin installing their refueling stations around the country.

It's Time for "Somebody" to Get Going . . .

As the old saying goes, "This ain't rocket science."

Perhaps now that the focus on healthcare reform is behind us, we can get back to the business of addressing the rest of America's crucial issues. And undoubtedly, increasing our energy independence is one of them.

Unlike crude oil, the United States is awash in natural gas. We have nearly 2,100 tcf (Trillion Cubic Feet), which equates to a 100-year supply.

The crude oil import problem reminds me of the old joke about "*Everybody, Somebody, Anybody and Nobody.*"

- *Everybody* thinks ending our dependence on foreign oil needs to be done.

- *Somebody* will do it.

- *Anybody* could put a plan together to end our dependence.

- But *Nobody* has.

The U.S. government needs to step up and be that *Somebody*.

My scenario is a simple way to solve it . . . right now. But we'll never get there if we don't get started.

C'mon, Congress . . . wake up. . . .

Why Natural Gas?

Unlike crude oil, the United States is awash in natural gas. We have nearly 2,100 tcf (Trillion Cubic Feet), which equates to a 100-year supply. That's 33% higher than just three years ago.

And you can bet that figure will rise further. In fact, with technological improvements, I fully expect that estimate to double over the next three to five years.

So how much gas do we need? One trillion cubic feet is enough to run 12 million cars per year. Replace 75% of the U.S. vehicle fleet (190 million vehicles) and we're still only talking 15 tcf per year.

While electric cars might be the ultimate alternative to fossil fuels, switching to natural gas-powered vehicles gets us a long way down the road towards energy independence.

More importantly, it buys America valuable time to replace power generation with alternatives, further reducing our dependence on fossil fuels.

The United States Must Increase Fuel Efficiency Standards

Jonathan Murray

Jonathan Murray, a veteran of the US Marines, is the former advocacy director for the Truman National Security Project, a national security leadership institute, and the former campaign director for Operation Free, a coalition of veterans and national security organizations that advocates for government action on climate change.

Congress is known for producing lots of "hot air." If some senators and representatives have their way during the new [2011] Congress, "hot air" could literally be the result of their work.

Certain senators and the new Republican-controlled House are attacking the Environmental Protection Agency's [EPA] authority to limit carbon pollution. This is likely to have devastating consequences for our environment and our national security.

National Security and Oil

Over the past 14 months, Operation Free and thousands of veterans across the country, from every generation, have worked to support a national clean energy policy. The Veterans for American Power tour visited hundreds of communities nationwide, meeting with thousands of Americans to deliver the message that U.S. national security is closely tied to our energy policy.

Jonathan Murray, "Climate Change: Next Security Threat," *Politico*, January 3, 2011. www.politico.com. Copyright © 2011 by Jonathan Murray. All rights reserved. Reproduced by permission.

In Washington, veterans have met with scores of senators to ask for support for a climate and energy policy that reduces dependence on oil.

This oil dependence is among the most dangerous threats to U.S. national security. For years, senior military and intelligence officials have warned that too much of U.S. oil payments eventually trickle down to terrorists, who use it to buy the weapons used against our troops in Afghanistan and Iraq.

Ignoring all the warnings and security implications, the Senate failed to consider comprehensive climate and energy legislation last session.

Former CIA Director Jim Woolsey said it best: "This [the war on terror] is the first time since the Civil War where we are funding both sides of the war."

The Threat of Climate Change

Ignoring all the warnings and security implications, the Senate failed to consider comprehensive climate and energy legislation last session. To make matters worse, Congress will soon consider legislation to strip the EPA of its authority under the Clean Air Act. This would give polluters' free reign to emit as much carbon pollution as they want, speeding up the effects of climate change and risking national security.

If climate change continues unchecked, we will see millions of people displaced globally, countries destabilized and U.S. troops mobilized to address these new threats.

The Defense Department calls climate change a destabilizing influence and "threat multiplier." There is no better example of climate change as a destabilizing force than what happened in Pakistan last year [2010]. More than one-fifth of Pakistan was flooded by torrential rains and insurgents have pounced on the chaos-created opportunity to turn Pakistan into a breeding ground and safe haven for terrorist activity.

As predicted climate-related calamities occur—including drought and famine in unstable countries like Somalia, Sudan and Yemen—these are also likely to become breeding grounds for terror.

Fuel Efficiency Standards

While some senators attempt to move us in the wrong direction, the [Barack] Obama administration now has an opportunity to steer us back on track. Pushed by a diverse coalition that includes veterans and national security organizations, the EPA recently set new fuel efficiency standards of 60 miles per gallon by 2025.

Sixty miles per gallon by 2025 is an achievable goal that we must attain if we are to reduce dependence on oil and strengthen our national security. It will significantly cut demand for oil and drive prices down.

And by reducing the $1 billion a day that the United States spends on importing oil, the new standard would put less money into the pockets of Iranian leader Mahmoud Ahmadinejad, his nuclear program and his recently developed "Ambassador of Death" missile. It would also significantly hamper other regimes seeking to do us harm.

Most Americans don't think about climate change as a national security threat. But we must begin to focus on how it makes us vulnerable in a global context. Thousands of veterans, active duty troops, intelligence professionals and national security experts are doing this every day—and will continue the fight to secure America with clean energy.

It is in our national security interest to do so.

The Free Market, Rather Than Government, Should Govern Energy Choices

Conn Carroll

Conn Carroll is the assistant director for strategic communications for the Heritage Foundation, a conservative think tank, and he is the editor of The Foundry, *the organization's policy blog.*

Last Friday [January 28, 2011] on a conference call with reporters about the [Barack] Obama Administration's long-term energy proposals, Energy Secretary Steven Chu responded to a question about the situation in Egypt, saying: "Certainly any disruption in the Middle East means a partial disruption in the oil we import. It's a world market and [a disruption] could actually have real harm of the price. The best way America can protect itself against these incidents is to decrease our dependency on foreign oil, in fact to diversify our supply." This is a nice sentiment. Unfortunately, everything the Obama Administration is doing is only increasing our dependence on foreign sources of oil.

Blocking Oil Production and Promoting Energy Taxes

Secretary Chu is right: Oil does sell on a world market. But transportation and other distribution factors do segment oil markets somewhat. In fact, the United States is currently paying about $10 less for a barrel of oil than European and Asian nations are. Why? Because of U.S. access to oil refined from Canadian oil sands. Access to these vast natural resources is a great diversification of our oil supply. But now the Obama Administration is trying to make it harder for American consumers to get Canadian oil. The Obama Environmental Protection Agency [EPA] is stonewalling approval for the Keystone pipeline, which would increase the amount of oil the U.S. receives from Canada by over a million barrels per day. And that is not the only oil the Obama Administration is trying to keep out of American consumers' hands.

Offshore, the Obama Interior Department has blocked access to 19 billion barrels of oil in the Pacific and Atlantic coasts and the eastern Gulf of Mexico—and another 10 billion barrels estimated in the Chukchi Sea off the Alaskan coast. Onshore, federal leasing of oil and gas exploration in the western United States has dropped significantly in the past two years. According to data compiled by the Western Energy Alliance, the Bureau of Land Management offered 79 percent fewer leases for oil and natural gas development in Colorado, Montana, New Mexico, North Dakota, Utah, and Wyoming in 2010 than in 2005. And then there is the Arctic National Wildlife Reserve, where an estimated 10 billion barrels of oil lie beneath a few thousand acres that can be accessed with minimal environmental impact.

> *Government policies that ban economically feasible energy development while subsidizing economically unsustainable ones only raise energy costs.*

Allowing Americans to develop these resources could easily produce at least 1 million new barrels of oil a day. The Heritage Foundation's Center for Data Analysis estimates that, if the United States managed to increase its domestic oil production by 1 million barrels a day, it would create an additional 128,000 jobs and generate $7.7 billion in economic activity.

As bad as these existing energy policies are, President Obama's planned energy policies are even worse. Today, the President is meeting with Senate Energy and Natural Resources Chairman Jeff Bingaman (D-NM) to plot passage of a clean energy standard (CES) bill. CES is just another cap-and-trade, energy-tax-like policy, except it's all cap and no trade. A CES would mandate that all electricity providers generate a certain percentage of energy from carbon-free sources. Just like cap and trade, this policy is fundamentally just an energy tax that would drive up everyone's electricity prices. Ironically, this would make electric vehicles even more expensive to operate, but we're sure the Obama Administration would offer another round of taxpayer-funded subsidies to fix that problem.

A Free-Market Approach

Government policies that ban economically feasible energy development while subsidizing economically unsustainable ones only *raise* energy costs rather than lowering them. What the U.S. economy really needs is a truly free-market energy approach, one that includes (1) real nuclear energy reform, not more loan guarantees; (2) predictable and sensible coal regulations; (3) reduced regulation on renewable energy; (4) an end to all energy subsidies; and (5) common-sense limits to environmental litigation.

Congress should not let unrest in the Middle East scare them into energy policies that would make all our energy only more expensive. More bans on energy development, more subsidies for economically unproven technologies, and expensive new alternative energy production mandates are not the answer. America needs a true free-market approach to energy, and we need it now.

Organizations to Contact

The editors have compiled the following list of organizations concerned with the issues debated in this book. The descriptions are derived from materials provided by the organizations. All have publications or information available for interested readers. The list was compiled on the date of publication of the present volume; the information provided here may change. Be aware that many organizations take several weeks or longer to respond to inquiries, so allow as much time as possible.

Cato Institute
1000 Massachusetts Ave. NW, Washington, DC   20001-5403
(202) 842-0200 • fax: (202) 842-3490
website: www.cato.org

Cato Institute is a nonprofit public policy research foundation that promotes a libertarian point of view that emphasizes principles of limited government, free markets, individual liberty, and peace. One of Cato's research areas is energy and the environment. Cato is committed to protecting the environment without sacrificing economic liberty, and the organization believes that those goals are mutually supporting, not mutually exclusive. Recent publications include *Oil Speculators Are Your Friends* and *The Case Against Government Intervention in Energy Markets*.

Center for Climate and Energy Solutions (C2ES)
2101 Wilson Blvd., Suite 550, Arlington, VA   22201
(703) 516-4146 • fax: (703) 516-9551
website: www.c2es.org

The Center for Climate and Energy Solutions (C2ES) succeeds the Pew Center on Global Climate Change, which was established in 1998 as a nonprofit, nonpartisan, and independent organization whose mission was to provide credible information, straight answers, and innovative solutions in the effort to address global climate change. In November 2011, the Pew Center was reestablished as the Center for Climate and Energy Solutions. The Center's website is an excellent source of publications, reports, fact sheets, articles, and speeches on all facets of the energy/climate change issue.

Environmental Literacy Council

1625 K St. NW, Suite 1020, Washington, DC   20006-3868
(202) 296-0390 • fax: (202) 822-0991
e-mail: info@enviroliteracy.org
website: www.enviroliteracy.org

The Environmental Literacy Council is an independent non-profit organization that helps teachers, students, policymakers, and the public find cross-disciplinary resources on the environment. The Council offers free background information on common environmental science concepts; vetted resources to broaden understanding; and curricular materials that give teachers the tools to augment their own backgrounds on environmental issues. The website contains a section on energy that provides information, recommended resources, and lesson plans relating to petroleum and US energy policies.

The Heritage Foundation

214 Massachusetts Ave. NE, Washington, DC   20002-4999
(202) 546-4400
website: www.heritage.org

The Heritage Foundation is a conservative think tank that promotes conservative public policies based on the principles of free enterprise, limited government, individual freedom, traditional American values, and a strong national defense. The group's staff conducts research on key policy issues and advocates conservative positions to members of Congress, congressional staff, policymakers in the executive branch, the news media, the academic community, and the public. Among the topics listed on the group's website is "Energy and Environment," a portal that leads to many articles and opinion pieces relating to fossil fuels, including, for example, *What to Do About High Oil Prices* and *Alternative Fuels as a Military Strategy.*

Institute for the Study of Energy and Our Future (ISEOF)
PO Box 270762, Fort Collins, CO   80527-0762
(303) 942-6209
e-mail: iseof.org
website: www.iseof.org

The Institute for the Study of Energy and Our Future (ISEOF) is a nonprofit corporation that conducts research and educates the public about energy issues and their impact on society. It publishes *The Oil Drum*, an online periodical devoted to discussions about energy and our future. According to the website, the world is near the point where new oil production cannot keep up with increased energy demand and older oil fields are nearly depleted, resulting in a decline of total world oil production. The website is an excellent source of analysis, research, and discussion of energy-related topics, such as peak oil, sustainable development and growth, and the implications of these ideas on politics.

International Energy Agency (IEA)
9 rue de la Fédération, 75739 Paris   Cedex 15
   France
+33 1 40 57 65 00/01 • fax: +33 1 40 57 65 09
e-mail: info@iea.org
website: www.iea.org

The International Energy Agency (IEA) is an intergovernmental organization that acts as energy policy advisor to twenty-eight member countries in their effort to ensure reliable, affordable, and clean energy for their citizens. Founded during the oil crisis of 1973–74, the IEA's initial role was to coordinate measures in times of oil supply emergencies, but that mandate has broadened to include promoting energy security, economic development, and environmental protection. The IEA's current work focuses on climate change policies, market reform, energy technology collaboration, and outreach to major consumers and producers of energy, such as China, India, Russia, and the OPEC countries. Publications available from IEA include *Energy Technology Transitions for Industry* and *Transport, Energy and CO₂: Moving towards Sustainability*.

Natural Resources Defense Council (NRDC)
40 West 20th St., New York, NY   10011
(212) 727-2700 • fax: (212) 727-1773
website: www.nrdc.org

Founded in 1970, the Natural Resources Defense Council (NRDC) is one of the nation's oldest environmental advocacy organizations. With a staff of more than three hundred and fifty lawyers, scientists, and policy experts, NRDC works to protect the planet's wildlife and wild places and to ensure a safe and healthy environment for all living things. Among the issues on NRDC's agenda are: curbing global warming, getting toxic chemicals out of the environment, moving America beyond oil, reviving our oceans, saving wildlife and wild places, and helping China go green. The group publishes a monthly newsletter, and the NRDC website is a good source of information about clean energy options. The website's energy section, for example, contains informative articles such as *Domestic Oil Drilling: Still Not a Solution to Rising Gas Prices*; *Grasping Green Car Technology*; *High Gas Prices: Supply and Demand*; and *Fighting Oil Addiction*.

Post Carbon Institute
613 4th St., Suite 208, Santa Rosa, CA   95404
(707) 823-8700 • fax: (866) 797-5820
website: www.postcarbon.org

The Post Carbon Institute is a nonprofit organization that helps individuals and communities understand and respond to the environmental, societal, and economic crises created by our dependence on fossil fuels. The group believes that world oil production has peaked and it aims to facilitate the process of transitioning to a more sustainable, post-carbon world. The group publishes the monthly *Post Carbon Newsletter*, featuring the latest news and information, and its website is a good source of articles, commentaries, reports, and books relating to oil depletion and the future of oil, energy, and the economy.

Resources for the Future (RFF)

1616 P St. NW, Suite 600, Washington, DC   20036
(202) 328-5000 • fax: (202) 939-3460
website: www.rff.org

Resources for the Future (RFF) is a nonprofit and nonpartisan organization that conducts independent research—rooted primarily in economics and other social sciences—on environmental, energy, natural resource, and public health issues. RFF was created at the recommendation of William Paley, then head of the Columbia Broadcasting System, who had chaired a presidential commission that examined whether the United States was becoming overly dependent on foreign sources of important natural resources and commodities. Today, one of the group's main areas of focus is energy and climate change. Examples of RFF publications include *An Economic Assessment of Eliminating Oil and Gas Company Tax Preferences* and *The Challenge of Climate for Energy Markets*.

US Department of Energy (DOE)

1000 Independence Ave. SW, Washington, DC   20585
(202) 586-5000 • fax: (202) 586-4403
e-mail: The.Secretary@hq.doe.gov
website: http://energy.gov

The US Department of Energy is the main federal agency responsible for ensuring America's security and prosperity by addressing its energy, environmental, and nuclear challenges through transformative science and technology solutions. The DOE website is a useful source of information about issues such as America's readiness to respond to oil disruptions, the national Strategic Petroleum Reserve, emerging technologies, and energy efficiency.

US Energy Information Administration (EIA)

1000 Independence Ave. SW, Washington, DC 20585
(202) 586-8800
e-mail: infoCtr@doe.gov
website: www.eia.gov

The US Energy Information Administration (EIA) is the statistical agency of the US Department of Energy (DOE) and is the nation's main source of unbiased energy data, analysis, and forecasting. Its mission is to provide policy-neutral data, forecasts, and analyses to promote sound policy making, efficient markets, and public understanding regarding energy and its interaction with the economy and the environment. The EIA website is a source of various reports and publications, such as *Petroleum Supply Monthly*, *Monthly Energy Review*, the *Annual Energy Review*, the *Short-Term Energy Outlook*, and the *Annual Energy Outlook*.

World Energy Council (WEC)

Regency House, 1-4 Warwick St., 5th Floor
London W1B 5LT
   United Kingdom
(+44 20) 7734 5996 • fax: (+44 20) 7734 5926
e-mail: info@worldenergy.org
website: www.worldenergy.org

The World Energy Council (WEC) is the foremost multi-energy organization in the world today. WEC has member committees in nearly one hundred countries, including most of the largest energy-producing and energy-consuming nations. Established in 1923, the organization's mission is to promote the sustainable supply and use of energy for the greatest benefit of all people. Examples of WEC publications include *Assessment of Energy Policy and Practices*, *Energy Efficiency Policies*, and *Europe's Vulnerability to Energy Crisis*.

Bibliography

Books

Robert U. Ayres and Edward H. Ayres
Crossing the Energy Divide: Moving from Fossil Fuel Dependence to a Clean-Energy Future. Philadelphia: Wharton School Publishing, 2009.

Daniel B. Botkin
Powering the Future: A Scientist's Guide to Energy Independence. Upper Saddle River, NJ: FT Press, 2010.

Robert Bryce
Gusher of Lies: The Dangerous Delusions of "Energy Independence." New York: PublicAffairs, 2009.

Committee on Assessment of Resource Needs for Fuel Cell and Hydrogen Technologies and National Research Council
Transitions to Alternative Transportation Technologies—Plug-in Hybrid Electric Vehicles. Washington, DC: National Academies Press, 2010.

Council on Foreign Relations
The New Arab Revolt: What Happened, What It Means, and What Comes Next. Washington, DC: Council on Foreign Relations/Foreign Affairs, 2011.

Dan Dicker
Oil's Endless Bid: Taming the Unreliable Price of Oil to Secure Our Economy. Hoboken, NJ: Wiley, 2011.

Bradley L. Dunne   *Corporate Average Fuel Economy (CAFE) Standards and the Environmental Impact.* Hauppauge, NJ: Nova Science, 2011.

Y Ev   *Electric Vehicle EV, the Second Coming: What You Need to Know to "Go Green & Go Electric."* Charleston, SC: CreateSpace, 2011.

Philip G. Gallman   *Green Alternatives and National Energy Strategy: The Facts Behind the Headlines.* Baltimore, MD: The Johns Hopkins University Press, 2011.

Newt Gingrich and Vince Haley   *Drill Here, Drill Now, Pay Less: A Handbook for Slashing Gas Prices and Solving Our Energy Crisis.* Washington, DC: Regnery Publishing, 2008.

Michael J. Graetz   *The End of Energy: The Unmaking of America's Environment, Security, and Independence.* Cambridge, MA: The MIT Press, 2011.

Christopher B. Hummel   *Plug-in Hybrid Electric Vehicles and Energy Use.* Hauppauge, NY: Nova Science, 2011.

Antonia Juhasz   *The Tyranny of Oil: The World's Most Powerful Industry—and What We Must Do to Stop It.* New York: Harper Paperbacks, 2009.

Anne Korin and Gal Luft — *Turning Oil into Salt: Energy Independence Through Fuel Choice.* Charleston, SC: BookSurge Publishing, 2009.

Roger E. Meiners — *The False Promise of Green Energy.* Washington, DC: Cato Institute, 2011.

Kent Moors — *The Vega Factor: Oil Volatility and the Next Global Crisis.* Hoboken, NJ: Wiley, 2011.

Malcom R. Perdontis — *Battery Manufacturing and Electric and Hybrid Vehicles.* Hauppauge, NY: Nova Science, 2011.

Joseph M. Shuster — *Beyond Fossil Fools: The Roadmap to Energy Independence by 2040.* Edina, MN: Beaver's Pond Press, 2008.

Christopher Steiner — *$20 Per Gallon: How the Inevitable Rise in the Price of Gasoline Will Change Our Lives for the Better.* New York: Grand Central Publishing, 2009.

Periodicals and Internet Sources

American Public Transportation Association — "Potential Impact of Gasoline Price Increases on U.S. Public Transportation Ridership, 2011–2012," March 14, 2011. www.apta.com.

E. Calvin Beisner   "Natural Gas a Natural Winner? Let the (Transportation) Market Decide!" *MasterResource*, May 24, 2011. www.masterresource.org.

Meteor Blades   "Think Big: Transportation Overhaul Would Save Money, Create Jobs, Cut Pollution, Burn Less Oil," *Daily Kos*, June 19, 2011. www.dailykos.com.

Ben Casselman   "Facing Up to End of 'Easy Oil,'" *Wall Street Journal*, May 24, 2011. http://online.wsj.com.

Gordon G. Chang   "Oil Shock," *Forbes*, February 27, 2011. http://blogs.forbes.com.

Rory Cooper   "10 Things You Need to Know About High Gas Prices and Obama's Oil Policy," *The Foundry*, February 23, 2011. http://blog.heritage.org.

Anthony H. Cordesman   "US Oil and Gas Import Dependence: Department of Energy Projections in 2011," Center for Strategic & International Studies, April 29, 2011. http://csis.org.

Aaron Couch   "Poll: With Gas Prices High, Americans Want 60 m.p.g. Fuel Efficiency," *Christian Science Monitor*, May 16, 2011. www.csmonitor.com.

Tanya Davis   "The Effect of Rising Gas Prices on American Families," Cmvlive.com, June 2, 2011. http://cmvlive.com.

The Economist   "The Gas-Price Debate," May 1, 2011. www.economist.com/blogs.

Jim Efstathiou Jr. and Kim Chipman	"Fracking: The Great Shale Gas Rush," *Bloomberg Businessweek*, March 3, 2011. www.businessweek.com.
Judah Flum	"Benefits to High Gas Prices?" JudahFlum.com, March 7, 2011. www.judahflum.com.
Merrill Goozner	"Oil Dependency: The Real Threat to National Security," *The Fiscal Times*, June 23, 2011. www.thefiscaltimes .com.
The Guardian	"Oil Prices: Green Light from the Black Stuff," March 5, 2011. www.guardian.co.uk.
Steve Hargreaves	"Gas Prices High—and Might Get Higher," *CNN Money*, January 21, 2011. http://money.cnn.com.
Ron Haynes	"12 Reasons Why High Gas Prices Are GOOD for America," *The Wisdom Journal*, May 13, 2008. www.thewisdomjournal.com.
The Independent	"An Opportunity to Kick Our Fossil-Fuel Addiction," January 6, 2011. www.independent.co.uk.
Jennifer Kho	"What High Gas Prices Mean for Renewable Energy," *Renewable Energy World*, May 31, 2011. www.renewable energyworld.com.
Clifford Krauss	"Can We Do Without the Mideast?" *New York Times*, March 30, 2011.

David Kreutzer | "Alternative Fuels as a Military Strategy," The Heritage Foundation, July 20, 2011. www.heritage.org.

Rebecca Lefton and Daniel J. Weiss | "Oil Dependence Is a Dangerous Habit: Imports Threaten Our Security, Our Environment, and Our Economy," Center for American Progress, January 2010. www .americanprogress.org.

Ben Levisohn | "Sizing Up the New Oil Spike," *Bloomberg Businessweek*, June 1, 2009.

David MacKay | "Let's Get Real About Alternative Energy," *CNN*, May 13, 2009. www.cnn.com.

Jason Mick | "FedEx CEO: 'Addiction' to Foreign Oil Is Costing the Economy, American Lives," *Daily Tech*, May 20, 2011. www.dailytech.com.

New Scientist | "High Fuel Prices Could Slash US Emissions," May 8, 2008.

Cullen Roche | "How Serious Is the Oil Price Threat to the US Recovery?" *Business Insider*, January 5, 2011. www.businessinsider .com.

Nansen G. Saleri | "Our Man-Made Energy Crisis," *Wall Street Journal*, March 9, 2011. http://online.wsj.com.

Julia A. Seymour   "Rising Gas Prices Linked to Obama Drilling Ban in Just 1% of Evening News Stories," Business & Media Institute, April 19, 2011. www.mrc .org.

Time   "Getting Transit to Work," May 12, 2011.

Michael Totty and Spencer Swartz   "How to Kick Our Oil Addiction Despite Plunging Oil Prices," *Wall Street Journal*, March 1, 2009. http:// online.wsj.com.

Index

A

Advanced Research Projects Agency-Energy (ARPA-E), 127
Afghanistan, 41, 144, 153
Ahmadinejad, Mahmoud, 38–39, 154
Air pollution
air quality rules, 58, 77
clean air programs, cost, 78–80
from fossil fuels, 18, 26, 128
high-speed rail and, 91
reduced oil consumption, 32, 145
standards for, 33–34
Air Resources Board, 78
Al Taie, Jaafar, 48–49
Alaska oil drilling, 62
Alaskan Wildlife Preserve (Arctic National Wildlife Preserve), 84
Algae fuels, 140
Algeria, 18, 43
Alternate energy sources, 82–84, 87
Amalgamated Transit Union, 118
American Petroleum Institute (API), 58, 63, 69, 132
American Public Transportation Association (APTA)
diesel fuel costs, 100
federal funding cuts and, 117–118
public transit investments needed, 95, 97–98, 101

American Recovery and Reinvestment Act of 2009 (ARRA), 126–128
Amtrak, 91, 92
Angola, 18
Arab-Israeli War, 21–22
Arab Spring uprising, 24, 47, 60
Arctic National Wildlife Reserve, 156
Arya, Atul, 60, 63
Association of Public Transportation Agencies, 112
Australia, 51
Ayatollah Khomeni, 23

B

Bahrain, 131
Banta, Henry, 71
Barker, J. Barry, 113
Barry, Sean, 94–96
BART trains (San Francisco, CA), 100
Bicycling, 94, 95
Bingaman, Jeff, 78, 157
Biofuels
algae fuels, 140
development of, 126, 127
increased use of, 63
investment in, 140
Verdezyne (yeast fuel), 140
Birol, Fatih, 60
Black carbon gas, 25
Bloomberg (newspaper), 72
Boehner, John, 119
BP oil company, 68, 128